Growing in Christian Maturity

How to Flow in
the Gifts of the Spirit

Growing in Christian Maturity

How to Flow in the Gifts of the Spirit

Herman H. Riffel

Destiny Image® Publishers, Inc.
P.O. Box 310
Shippensburg, PA 17257-0310

"Speaking to the Purposes of God for this Generation
and for the Generations to Come"

ISBN 1-56043-191-1
(Previously published as *Christian Maturity* by
Bethany Fellowship, Inc., ISBN 0-87123-059-3)

Library of Congress Catalog Card Number: 97-65738

For Worldwide Distribution
Printed in the U.S.A.

This book and all other Destiny Image, Revival Press,
and Treasure House books are available
at Christian bookstores and distributors worldwide.

For a U.S. bookstore nearest you, call **1-800-722-6774**.
For more information on foreign distributors, call **717-532-3040**.
Or reach us on the Internet: **http://www.reapernet.com**

Dedication

To Lillie, my wife,
who has been a constant encouragement to me,
who shared in the fellowship of learning, and
who now shares generously in the ministry.

Contents

Preface

The material in this book has been given as lectures, approximately 50 times in 16 countries. The eager response, from almost 1200 Protestant missionaries in many countries, from priests and nuns in Rome, and from Orthodox believers in Athens, has persuaded me that this subject does have a universal appeal to those who are spiritually hungry. Amazingly, I have been able to present these lectures to American and Canadian university professors with the same response as from African pastors, who are only a few years away from witchcraft. But of more importance than the immediate response is the change that we have been able to see, or to learn about, in the lives of so many who have received these messages.

However, I recognize that this material is only a segment of neglected teaching, and that it needs to be put into a balance with all else that we find in the sacred Scriptures. This material is presented to fill a gap of teaching for those who have learned that power is available for ministry by the Holy Spirit, but they do not know how to avoid the pitfalls of immaturity when they do receive this power. The Jerusalem Bible is used by the permission of the editors, but I encourage the reader to compare the texts carefully with other translations. Time and place, relating to persons we were seeking to help through counseling and prayer, have often been altered in order to keep their identity secret.

I wish to express my deep appreciation to many in Ontario, Canada: Drs. Glyn and Helen Reesor of Waterloo who provided a secluded place for writing; Bob and Eva Macleod of Kitchener who supplied secretarial and other detailed help; Dr. Douglas Lowry, professor at Waterloo Lutheran University and pastor of St. David's Presbyterian Church of Campbellville, who carefully edited all the material; Fr. Francis Martin of Combermere, a great student of the Scriptures and professor at the Gregorian University in Rome, who edited all the material and gave many valuable suggestions. I am also grateful to these in the United States: professors from Michigan State University and other universities, who edited certain chapters and gave excellent counsel; Sr. Margaret Sullivan, who corrected the earlier revisions for grammar and expression; and to many, many others who gave valuable help and undergirded this work with prayer.

It is my prayer that the same liberating effect that has come to so many listeners will come to many more readers, even while we are still learning about the power of God, which is so real and so available to us today.

H.H.R.

Chapter 1

Mature Personhood

A couple called from the hospital, obviously upset. Their seven-year-old boy, Kenny, had previously been checked for eye trouble. The doctors now told the parents that he was suffering from a malignant brain tumor. He was not expected to live more than two or three months. There was nothing the doctors could do except give cobalt treatments that could not heal but would, at best, temporarily arrest the cancer. The parents said they had thought of taking their boy to a church that had healing meetings, but since such a consideration was contrary to their previous religious training, they came instead to me, as their pastor, saying, "If God can heal there, then He can heal here." So they laid the problem at my feet. What was I to do as a pastor who had previously referred all healing to the doctors? This time the doctors were helpless. Could I just send them away to others who believed what I had been taught not to believe?

About the same time a young man who was very close to our family was in deep trouble. I had given counsel many times before, and now I had the opportunity of advising again. I said, "God can help you." The response was a simple phrase, "Oh yeah?" That cut to my heart.

I suddenly was aware that my words were theory. As long as I only had to say, "God can help you," I was sending the needy ones to find their own help in God. I later learned it was when I would say, "I can help you," that I could do anything for the one in need. Of course, the help has to come from God, and I am only the channel of His power. But unless I could pray the prayer of faith that can deliver, I remained in utter helplessness. It was imperative for me to find out how God wants to work, and learn to cooperate with Him.

I had good home training in which I came to know Christ personally, and I began early to develop my own devotional life. I had undergone preparation for the ministry in which the Scriptures were diligently taught. Why, after this and 20 years in the pastoral, had I come to the end of myself? I could not deceive myself, for I knew that my Christian experience was not sufficient for me to be able to respond, "*I can help you.*" But as I looked around me, I did not see a Christianity that was any greater. I would compare myself with others and come off fairly well, but that was not sufficient to meet desperate needs.

Christianity, as I saw it on that day, was as insignificant to the world situation as many of its detractors had always said. I would have to give it all up or find something in Christianity that I had not yet found. What I had found thus far was real, but it was not sufficient. My growth and discovery had stopped somewhere short of the needs that surrounded me.

2

At the time this young man came to me with his need, I had come a long way from an early childhood experience of deep conviction of sin and repentance, followed by a sudden knowledge that I, indeed, did believe and was a child of God. My conversion experience did not fit any of the patterns that I was taught during my years of theological training. The formula for salvation had become so simple that I had told this boy all he needed to do was to ask Jesus to come into his life. He had done so, and then quickly helped his sister to do the same. But if the formula for salvation was simple and so sure, why did problems arise in his early teens and grow so rapidly, blossoming into revolt? In fact, I wondered why this happened to many young people who had made early decisions for Christ.

In my training and background, there had been much emphasis upon that great spiritual crisis in life called the new birth or conversion. This spiritual rebirth, or new birth, that Jesus referred to (see Jn. 3), we, of course, know to be essential to bring forth spiritual life. For as Jesus said, "What is born of the flesh is flesh; what is born of the Spirit is spirit. Do not be surprised when I say: You must be born from above" (Jn. 3:6-7). However, the way that this takes place within a person is not so easily defined. Jesus said, "The wind blows wherever it pleases; you hear its sound, but you cannot tell where it comes from or where it is going. That is how it is with all who are born of the Spirit" (Jn. 3:8).

Some churches place great emphasis upon the personal conversion experience. I believe that is right. However, if the emphasis is such that conversion becomes a formula, then the one trying the "formula" no longer has an experience of the "heart" but only of the mind, and no real birth takes place. It seems that this person must move from the conscious understanding to the involvement of the deep unconscious. With the mind, he needs to understand enough to help direct the will, but the response must come from the whole person—that is, the mind and the "heart."

Those churches that place great emphasis upon the symbolic acts of worship often have a long tradition to draw from. However, it seems evident that a long background of Christian tradition alone is not sufficient to ensure a personal faith in Christ. A man from this background must move from the unconscious inheritance of tradition to the conscious acceptance of Jesus Christ into his life. He is moving from the unconscious to the conscious experience with Christ, thus personally involving the whole man in a relationship with the Lord.

St. John tells us that though Jesus came into the world, many of "his own people did not accept him. But to all who did accept him he gave power to become children of God." Those that did this were "born not out of human stock or urge of the flesh or will of man but of God himself" (Jn. 1:11b-12a,13). The fact that these people that John speaks of had a great tradition as Jews was not enough. They had to personally and consciously receive and commit themselves to Jesus Christ. This is still true.

I had been taught that it was necessary to receive Jesus Christ personally into my life and commit myself to Him. However, the inference, if not the direct teaching, was that if just the decision was made to receive Jesus Christ into one's life, then all else would follow. It is true that we were also taught to strive to become good Christians, but this was on the basis of the *ought*. You ought to pray, and you ought to read your Bible, and you ought to do better. These oughts had great power to burden me with guilt and cause me to struggle, but no power to make me the kind of Christian I ought to be. So the unstated formula for Christian maturity was to get men saved through faith in Jesus Christ, and then trust legalistic obligations to bring them along to perfection.

I knew from experience that conversion is real, but I couldn't understand why so many turned away from that experience. The answer became clearer through a discussion I had with Dr. Paul Tournier, the great Christian psychiatrist and author from Geneva, Switzerland. As we spoke about the experience of conversion, he said, "The reason we differ is that you think of conversion as a single point, while I look at it as a lifetime experience." Then he went on to say that many Christians, even Christian leaders, come to him having "it," that is, an experience they call salvation; but they are filled with fears, tensions, anxieties, frustrations, and boredom. They have let Christ make their spirits alive, but they have not let Him fill their emotions and intelligence and wills. This crystalized my thinking on conversion.

I now see conversion as a process of converting the whole man to Jesus Christ. Thus, conversion is a lifetime process. The *spiritual new birth is* the *first conscious relationship* with God through Christ. This is, however, only the *first step* in conversion. People *must* have a *spiritual birth* to enter the Kingdom of God, just as one must have a physical birth to enter the natural life. Jesus replied: "I tell you most solemnly, unless a man is born through water and the Spirit, he cannot enter the kingdom of God: what is born of the flesh is flesh; what is born of the Spirit is spirit" (Jn. 3:5). The Kingdom of God is a spiritual kingdom, and God, by His Spirit, makes His entrance into a person through a person's spirit.

People have attempted to bring about communication with God but have always failed. It is evident that a person cannot reach God through his body, i.e., no one can physically reach God by climbing into the heavens. Neither can people reach God through the soul, although much of religion is an attempt to do that. Some try to do it intellectually by building great doctrines, but no amount of theology can make us alive. Some try to reach God emotionally, but though they can produce a great deal of excitement or feeling, they cannot bring about spiritual life. Life originates with God. It comes from the Father, is manifest through the Son, and is communicated by the Spirit of God to our spirit, bringing about the spiritual new birth. This life then renews our minds and will even make our dying bodies live

$$God \begin{cases} Father \\ Son \\ Holy\ Spirit \end{cases}$$

$$Man \begin{cases} spirit \\ soul \\ body \end{cases}$$

again. Therefore, the "new birth" that Jesus spoke of is the reception of new life from God through personal repentance and faith in Jesus Christ.

As birth is the entrance to life, and growth continues from there on, so also the spiritual new birth is the entrance into the Kingdom of God, and conversion continues from that point on. God's will is not only that Jesus Christ enters the life of a person through his spirit, but that He occupies the whole person: spirit, soul, and body. This, to me, has become the process that I would call conversion. I recognized clearly that what I had been observing was true: namely, that the parents' continual focusing on their children's earlier decisions for Christ did not lead them into growth.

It is said that Charles Haddon Spurgeon, the great English preacher, accepted Jesus Christ into his life when he was four, and regarded this decision as valid all his lifetime. But what was valid for one person might not be valid for all. And, what is valid is not necessarily sufficient. The child at 12 to 14 years of age has come to realize that that which was valid for him at age six is not sufficient for him now. He has developed in areas that he did not know of before. This new part of himself, which he has discovered since the age of six or eight, must also be converted to Christ. In fact, conversion to Christ not only continues in the teens but goes on all through life.

We assume that the young man about to take on the responsibility of a home and family has matured from early teens. Is that maturity or responsibility to be directed only to his wife and family, or is it to be given to Christ? If his new abilities are to be directed only to the former, then he will be mature in his social and emotional relations but only a child in the spiritual. It is evident that this is true of many in the church. Conversion to Christ must not only have a real beginning; it must also continue to develop with every crisis period. When we stop converting our lives to Jesus Christ, we stop maturing, and boredom and restlessness are the result.

My experience as a hospital chaplain persuaded me that some Christians have been trapped at their very entrance to the Kingdom of God. I often illustrate this by comparing it to a house with many doors. We will call the first door *guilt*. The recognition of sin is a true and valid way of entrance into the Kingdom of God, for Jesus said, "Unless you repent, you will all perish" (see Lk. 13:3,5). However, when we insist that guilt is the only door through which Jesus enters our lives, we ignore the many other needs through which Jesus desires to come. In fact, to press all people to come to Jesus by proving their guilt may only impose guilt upon them. They may feel no guilt at all, but still feel other needs.

As a hospital chaplain, I found many people came to Jesus because they were afraid. As I stepped to a woman's bedside, she said, "I am having surgery tomorrow," but what she really meant was, "I am afraid." Then I said, "Whatever your past experience with God, there is an area or room of your life filled with fear, and we can invite Jesus Christ to come in and take away the fear." Thus, Jesus comes in through the door of fear. For me to say that the patient is a sinner, and to impose upon her a burden of guilt that she did not feel, may only confuse her and bring her to despair. Rather, I could help her to Jesus through the door of fear, and Jesus would really meet her there.

There are many needs that may bring a person to Christ. Some may come because of anxiety, some because of loneliness, and some because of sorrow, or sickness, or frustration, or emptiness of life. Through any of these doors of need, one may be brought directly to Jesus.

However, let us compare the experience of a man who has his guilt removed and the woman who found that Jesus took away fear. The man knew Jesus as the one who forgives sins. But did he know that He also takes away fear? Probably not, for that had not been his need at that time. The other knew Jesus as the deliverer from fear, but yet, had not become aware of the forgiveness of sin that Jesus can bring. We have only what we receive by faith. One received freedom from guilt; the other received freedom from fear. But does the conversion experience stop there, or has it just begun? Though the man is free from guilt, he must learn how Jesus also frees from fear. The woman freed from fear must learn how Jesus takes away guilt. We must allow Jesus to invade all the areas of our lives and fill the need; then we can identify with others' needs and better help them.

Thus, we grow from one experience of freedom to another, and so on, to maturity. The one who has never known the comfort that comes in sorrow cannot help the one who has just lost a loved one. As we allow the Lord to comfort us in our varying sorrows, free us from anxiety, lead us through frustrations, and fill the emptiness of our lives, we grow to maturity. We never can afford to stop growing in our experience, for there are always more needs to fill in our lives, and there is always more fulfillment to find in Jesus.

I remember a patient who, with a laugh, invited me into his hospital room. He recognized me as a hospital chaplain and told of another patient who had just been in his room trying to get him saved. He showed me some booklets that the former man had left, which proved to be Scripture portions. He said that the visitor surely knew the Bible and told him all kinds of things, even how we were going to go up in the clouds. "He even tried to persuade me to become a believer right now."

I thought perhaps this patient was a hard character. But after listening to him a minute, I said, "I believe that God answers prayer." I prayed briefly with him. I saw him several times after that, and then one day he invited me into his room and closed the door. He poured out his troubles to me. Perhaps, he had been waiting to tell the former visitor about them, but evidently, the visitor was too busy telling him the things that he thought the man ought to know instead of listening to his need. I had learned that if we will only listen, we will soon hear the real need, and through that door of need bring a friend to Jesus.

I am impressed that the aim of the New Testament teaching is to bring God's children into maturity; a maturity that includes a person's full acceptance and love of himself, of all others, and of God. Maturity is not an impossible goal for the future but a developing process of the body, soul, and spirit, so that at each level the person can take appropriate responsibility for life in all three realms, and can enter into maturity. The church has spent much of its efforts in bringing children into the family of God. It is evident that as a child must be born to enter this world, so must a person be born of the Spirit to enter the Kingdom of God. Jesus said, "In truth, in very truth I tell you, unless a man has been born over again he cannot see the Kingdom of God" (Jn. 3:3, NEB). But Jesus never stopped there in His teaching. When the man who had been wild, uncontrollable, and under demonic forces was set free, he was told to go home alone so that growth could begin (see Mk. 5:1-20). He wanted to stay with Jesus, as a little child prefers to stay with his mother, but Jesus immediately started him off to maturity.

The writers of the Epistles all looked toward the maturity of the believers. Paul says, "In this way we are all to come to unity in our faith and in our knowledge of the Son of God, until we become the perfect Man, fully mature with the fullness of Christ himself" (Eph. 4:13).

The difference between a child in a family and a mature son is that the son takes responsibility. The child asks and receives what the father chooses to give him, but the mature son is not content with this. He has learned to know what his father's purpose is, and he expects to receive what he asks for. He also is willing to take responsibility for his actions, right or wrong, and therefore can be given authority. It is the same in the family of God. But according to this measurement, how many mature sons and daughters have we in our churches? Are we not mostly children who do not know how to recognize the voice of God or to decide what the will of God is? Therefore, we cannot take responsibility; neither are we prepared for the awful authority given to the sons and daughters of God. It is time that we grow to maturity, so that we can accept the responsibility that Jesus gave to His Church, and put to use His authority. He said, "All authority in Heaven and earth is given to Me. Go therefore...," implying, "go with this authority" (Mt. 28:18-19). But this kind of authority demands maturity.

The barriers to maturity may be many, but after traveling around the world speaking to many in the Christian ministry, I found that the obstacles to my growth were basically the same as those that have stunted the growth of the whole evangelical church. Some of the barriers have arisen because of our denominational doctrines. It was interesting to me that some psychologists dislike doctrinal formulas, because they feel such doctrinal formulas are nothing but crystallized experience. When something is crystallized, it is dead. For example, we are guilty of implying that because Luther had a certain experience, all Lutherans should have that same experience. Calvin experienced his salvation in terms of a certain emphasis; since his time, many doctrines have been built so that all Calvinists may experience the same. So, each denomination has doctrines that have crystallized into the pattern of someone's great experience.

If the personal experiences or charisma of individual believers, great though they are, are imposed upon others, they become binding. The farmers in Midwest United States had a saying that corn should be knee high by the Fourth of July, but fortunately they did not make it a doctrine. Thus, corn which was higher was not cut down, neither was corn which was shorter pulled out. They did not even have a conference to decide just how many inches "knee high" was. The saying was only a common standard to strive for. When the teachings of great people of the past can be treated as standards to strive for, and not as limitations to others whose experience is different, then doctrine too can be good.

In order to grow to maturity, we must allow for the development of the whole person. Personality may be defined as the motivating force coming from the body, soul, and spirit of the individual that determines his or her unique expression to the whole environment. "Christ to me is the full balance of the personality," an analyst said to me at the Carl Jung Institute for Analytical Psychology in Zurich, Switzerland. I realized there was a great truth in that statement when one recognized that only Jesus Christ can bring the personality into full balance.

Carl Jung divided *personality* into the now familiar forms of extrovert and introvert. The introvert lives by a world within him and is often uncomfortable in the world outside; for that reason, he often takes his stand against that which is public opinion. The extrovert lives by the world outside of him and is comfortable there. But for a person to be whole, Jung asserted, he must develop both sides of his personality. He must be able to live in both worlds. In fact, "Christ in us" is the only way that the full balance of the personality can be achieved. An enlightening study of how all personality traits are brought into balance in the life of Jesus is made in John A. Sanford's challenging book, *The Kingdom Within.*

There are many ways in which personality may be described. For example, in Jung's description of human behavior (in terms of thinking, feeling, sensation, and intuition) he says,

> "These four functional types correspond to the obvious means by which consciousness obtains its orientation to experience. Sensation (i.e., sense perception) tells you that something exists; thinking tells you what it is; feeling tells you whether it is agreeable or not; and intuition tells you whence it comes and where it is going."[1]

However, the person does not develop each function equally. In one person, thinking by logic and reasoning is developed strongly and provides a basis for his way of relating to others. Another finds emotions, through which she can please people and keep harmony, are most important in life. The person who sees clearly the world around her, having a strong sensory awareness, often feels that is all that needs to be taken into account. By contrast, the intuitive person "sees" an unseen world by which he may make

---

1.   Carl G. Jung et al., *Man and His Symbols* (New York, NY: Dell Publishing Co., 1964), 49.

the sensation-oriented person very uncomfortable. But to be whole, we need to bring Christ into all these areas.

It is not enough to know what orientation of personality we may have, but rather, we should know how Christ may enter into every area. If Christ is to occupy the whole person, we must allow Him to awaken in us those parts that are neglected. The logically oriented personality usually views the feeling function as a weakness. He cannot stand the person that "wears her feelings on her sleeves." However, that is so because he does not yet feel comfortable in making value judgments by feeling and would rather stay with the more familiar way of deciding by logic. He must defend himself against that which he is unsure of within himself and in others. Thus, he further loses his sensitivity to others and is unaware of the quality of the argument, so easily dismissed by him, offered by the feeling type of person. Yet, he wonders why people do not understand him. On the other hand, the one who is strongly feeling-oriented may make good and valid judgments, but is not able to fit them into the logic of time and practical arrangements. Therefore, she feels frustrated and is deeply hurt for not being understood. Both the thinking and feeling orientations are valid, but both persons must learn to recognize the value of the other by awakening the functions that are dormant within themselves.

Sensation and intuition-oriented persons often contrast each other in perceptive ability. The sensation-directed person thinks he sees everything, for his senses are alive to the trees and flowers, people, governments, and powers. He does not pass this world by without seeing it. However, the intuitively oriented person is aware of another unseen world, one which is just as real to her as the world that can be seen by the physical eyes. Thus, she makes the sensation-oriented person fairly groan in despair when she intuitively "feels" that something is wrong.

A group of American and Australian young people in Papua New Guinea were talking about an automobile accident in which they had been involved. One girl said that she "felt" that they should stop, for she sensed that something was going to go wrong. I asked the driver what he would have said if she had voiced her feelings. "I would have said that she was crazy," he said. I called their attention to the fact that if she would have persuaded them to stop and, thus, avoided the accident, he still would have had no proof. We often silence the intuitive voice and wonder why we have so much trouble.

A friend tells of canceling a plane reservation because she intuitively felt that there was something wrong. That plane crashed. When she told of this someone said, "Do you think that God was only interested in you and not in the others because you were the only one that received the warning?"

"No," she said, "God must have warned everyone, but they did not listen." Intuition is a natural ability given to all persons, but in our rational, extroverted world we have stilled this voice. Jesus Christ wants to speak through all our functions, but if we neglect to develop an area of the personality, we may not be able to understand Him as He speaks. Perhaps, as a member of a family, one fails to hear Christ speak through a spouse or through children. Conflicts in the home and the marriage relationship often result. If, however, we are awakened to the function that is opposite to ours in our partner, the marriage can be enriched, and each individual will grow thereby.

There is a great longing for maturity in people, who are all made in the image of the Creator. Just as the strongest force in physical life is for growth, so it is also in the spiritual. Our soul cries out when we remain unfulfilled, for God has made us to have full expression of our whole person. In fact, I have expressed the will of God to young people by saying, "The will of God for you is what you most want to do." Of course it is not what you want to do superficially, but *what your soul cries out for*. This is what many young people need to hear, because their conception of the will of God is a distorted one, implying that it must be painful, sad, sacrificial, and disappointing. Instead, it is the most fulfilling, satisfying experience of life, as the Psalmist said, "I delight to do thy will, O my God" (Ps. 40:3a, KJV). God has given us many creative abilities, and He wants them to be realized.

When part of a personality with its creative ability is unfulfilled, the soul cries out in ways that are often not understood. For example, men and women, single and married, have asked: "Why do I lust after or desire that man or woman? I do not really want him or her, but why do I have such strong sexual desires toward this person?" When asked if there was a longing for fulfillment in certain areas of expression, the answer was that the person questioned always wanted to write, but time did not permit. Or another might have wanted to pour out his soul in music, but he could not afford to buy an instrument. I say that their souls are crying out to be fulfilled!

God who is the Creator has made us to express ourselves creatively. The creative desires within us are manifold and come from deep within us, implanted there by God. These creative desires want expression, not only in music and art, but in many creative ways, such as creative building, or homemaking, or gardening, or administration, or research. If these creative desires are blocked and cannot find their proper expression, they will break out on a lower level. That is why Paul says that men who refuse to worship the Creator (and thus become like Him) have been given up by God to their sexual lusts (see Rom. 1); for with their refusal to worship God, they have denied themselves the fruit of worship—the creative expression of God's life within them. Hence, the drive towards life has broken out on a lower level. Hence, also, come those insistent drives, making the compulsive liar, thief, or gossip. The energy that is within us must find expression.

God has put these drives within us! Let us recognize that creative power is positive, and that a compulsive drive does not necessarily need to be negative, for it may be a misdirected energy within us. This drive may also come from wounds in our souls, for which we are applying tentative solutions—alcohol, drugs, or sex, which in turn can become compulsive drives in themselves. But if we apply these ad hoc ways of relieving some kind of tension, they engender greater tensions. We must recognize that the tension is correct, but instead of directing the energy into some compulsive solution, that only brings false healing, we must direct it into something deeper and more real. If we are troubled by a compulsive drive, let us thank God for the energy and ask Him to open up proper creative expressions for that which is now being misdirected by this drive.

The sexual relation in marriage is one proper fulfillment for the creative drive within us, but it is only one of many. In fact, the creative drives may find their expression in a single person without sexual relations as fully as in marriage. This is evident in some who have fulfilled their calling of God in abstinence, and yet have given great expression of creative fulfillment.

The varieties of creative expression are just as great as the patterns of the snowflake. Our educational system has limited us, giving very little emphasis upon creative fulfillment, and so many young people are seeking it in their own way. God wants us to break out of a narrow pattern that the "job qualification that offers the most money" has put upon us. No doubt our youth are rebelling against the unfulfilled lives of those who have achieved positions of wealth and prestige, but are left with empty lives. The Christian, above all, should be free to develop the creative abilities that lead to maturity and fulfillment.

A very important and long-range part of personal development is to bring more and more of the personality into consciousness, so that we can deal with it. The person, living under a mood, is allowing an energy out of his unconscious self to control him. He, thus, is not in conscious control and may be impelled suddenly to do an unpredictable thing. If he can examine the mood that is trying to overpower him, he can uncover the energy that is so powerfully depressing him. Then, with God's power, he can turn this energy into a creative expression for Christ.

To be mature is to be fully developed. Christian maturity is the development of the whole person, putting it all into subjection to Christ. There is no stopping the conversion process until the whole person—spirit, soul, and body—is fully converted to Christ. It does not matter through which door of need Jesus has entered. If we want to be able to meet the needs of others, then we must allow Him to meet their needs in our lives. More and more of the unconscious parts of ourselves must be brought into consciousness, so they can be subject to Christ and He can be Lord of all. Thus, we can fulfill the command of Jesus, "You must therefore be perfect just as your heavenly

Father is perfect" (Mt. 5:48). That word "perfect" means "complete," referring to our coming to completeness of maturity in Christ. This is not an impossible demand of sinless perfection, but rather an appeal that we grow in grace until we become fully "mature with the fullness of Christ himself."

In this day of the Holy Spirit's power, maturity is eminently needed in the Church. The Spirit is moving upon His people in all the world, and with the Spirit's stirring, there is a manifestation of power. Many are seeking such power, but power is dangerous if it is not directed by mature wisdom. The slander caused by the misuse of power has hurt the Church a great deal. Shall we then say, as some do, that we will have nothing to do with a power that can be misused? If so, we too are but children who are not ready to take responsibility. Many have been injured or have even lost their lives through the misuse of electrical power. Should we then have abolished its use, as some advocated at the beginning? How powerless would have been the machines that produce the products we depend on. So it is in the spiritual realm; except in this realm, we have to a great degree abolished the use of the Spirit's power, leaving a weak and frustrated Church. But the needs of the world are crowding in upon us. We cannot afford to grab for power, as children, or to reject it as too dangerous. We must become mature Christians to whom God can entrust responsibility and power.

I found that I, too, had been bound in areas of my life through the crystallization of some doctrines. To become mature, I had to let go of the structures that prevented creative expression within me. My new birth was real. I knew that by experience, as well as by scriptural teaching. However, I knew that the conversion process just began there and had to continue all through my lifetime. It was encouraging to know that compulsive drives were not bad in themselves, but contained emotional energy that could be directed into new, creative expressions. This thought opened up new doors for me. However, it involved many struggles, for old fears bound me to my former patterns of thinking. Though I, like Paul, knew what I ought to do, I could not do it. I had to find some means of release. It had to come through a means with which I was not yet acquainted. If Christ was sufficient for all problems, then I had to discover more of His power.

Questions for Discussion

1. How do people have communication with God?
2. What is the difference between the new birth and conversion? Describe the two experiences in your life.
3. What is Christian maturity? What measure of maturity have you found in your life?

Chapter 2

Healing of
the Inner Person

Maturity is important, but it is not easily obtained. My own struggles in life testified to that. From early childhood, I had developed a fear that would not allow me to relate freely to a certain type of person. As I went into the ministry, I developed ways of covering it up; but underneath, the fear was still at work. Unconsciously, it caused me a great deal of difficulty with the members of the church boards and committees. Though I prayed much about it, it held on, as if fastened by deep roots. I asked other Christians to pray for and with me, but the fear refused to give up its hold. It was many years before I heard a man tell of the healing of early memories. When I told him of my problem, he said, "Oh, that is simple!"

It was simple to him, for when he laid his hands on me and asked God to set me free from this fear, it was as though he pulled up a plant with the roots and all. He reached right into my childhood, and there asked the

21

Lord to take away the fear that had fastened itself to me. That was amazing!

When I heard of the healing of memories, it sounded so simple. "There is no past or future with God. Therefore we can ask Jesus to go back to the source of the problem in the life of the one we are seeking to help and expect God to meet it."

I was not yet familiar with the solid scriptural basis for this new truth, but it seemed right that through the death of Christ on the cross we should be set free from all bondages. Furthermore, I knew it had worked in my life as my friend prayed for me. It was not long before I could test it on the needs of others.

I was in another country when a woman came to our small group of believers who gathered to meet each other's needs. She asked for prayer for her son. He was 16 years old and very rebellious. There was nothing she could do with him; indeed, she had never had good communication with him. Her husband had, but he was in another country and would not be back for some months, and her need was urgent. I asked if I could pray with her, for she had already given the clue when she said that she had never had good communication with her son. I knew that there must be a barrier between them, as there sometimes is for reasons that are unknown to us. With some people we have an easy rapport, and with others, we find it difficult to communicate.

I do not know how this barrier arose between the mother and son, but she said that there never had been good communication between them. Sometimes we know that such a barrier can be received into one's mind by a word of prejudice or a difficult experience with another person. It can be carried for years and then projected on to to another person, even to one's own child. But we know that Jesus would remove all barriers between people. Could we believe that Jesus would remove all barriers between mother and son if we asked Him to? The mother, we knew, was honest before God in confession and obedience, and yet the barrier was there.

I laid my hands upon her and asked that Jesus go back in her life to the place or point of time where the barrier was first set up. We prayed in faith that this was being done and that Christ's work on the cross was being made effective in her at that moment, and we gave thanks to God for it. The next time we saw her she said that when she got home she found her son washing dishes, and they began to talk. They talked and talked until midnight that night and the next night, and the next.

A few weeks later the son came to talk to me about giving his life to Christ. Further evidence came about six months later. Her husband told how he had received letters telling of the many problems, and then the glowing report of what had happened through prayer. He had thought that the results would perhaps last a week or two, but instead, they had already lasted for six months.

After several years, the rapport established by the removal of the barrier was still there. We knew that this was the work of God. We had always believed that Jesus died to remove all barriers, but we had not exercised the authority that Jesus had given to us to remove them.

This was amazing, and gradually I learned the scriptural basis for the healing of memories. In the process of our development, we may find that our growth is being hindered and sense that we are bound by the experiences of the past. We get an occasional glimpse of a long-forgotten sorrow or hurt, and it haunts us as fear or threat whenever we determine to claim the freedom that is rightly ours. We apply all the means that God has made available for us to be forgiven, but we find that we cannot forgive or release ourselves. We become frustrated because we realize that it is not our sin that has bound us but the sin of others, through no fault of our own. Then we need the help of another who can speak the words of release with authority and power. Because there are so many bound by the past, we need to be able, not only to find our own help, but to help one another. As mature Christians, we need to be able to say, with authority in His name, what Jesus said of Himself in the synagogue in His hometown of Nazareth.

The spirit of the Lord has been given to me, for he has anointed me. He has sent me to bring the good news to the poor, to proclaim liberty to captives and to the blind new sight, to set the downtrodden free, to proclaim the Lord's year of favor (Luke 4:18-19).

First, let us consider how great is our privilege as Christians to confess our sins directly to God and be completely forgiven. Many do not know how quickly and effectively the guilt of their sins can be taken away by simply confessing their sins to God with the honest desire of leaving them. Much effort is spent in trying to minimize or ignore or forget sin, but ignoring it does not do away with its effect, even though the conscious memory of it may be gone for a time. Guilt or fear may indeed be buried in the unconscious only to express itself later as an illness, or some other problem, if we do not confess it and receive complete forgiveness.

As chaplains in the hospital, we learned from the doctors the process by which illness may come as a result of unconfessed sin. Let us suppose you say a word to me that I do not like, and I decide not to forgive it immediately. By deciding not to forgive, I have already given an order to my unconscious (i.e., that part of me that controls almost all the functions of the body without my being consciously aware of it) to hold on to this memory. This order is received by the autonomic nervous system, whereupon a constriction is placed upon the blood supply or nervous energy that normally flows to various organs of the body. Because these organs do not get their normal supply of energy they may send out a signal of pain. But they are not yet diseased, so when the doctor examines them he finds nothing wrong, even though I, the patient, feel intense pain. If the constriction is not removed by confession of the sin and the receiving of forgiveness, then some organ may become diseased, and medicine or surgery may need to be applied.

Such pain can also be caused by worry or tension, hatred or fear. The simple confession of these sins to God can set us completely free from them and from their physical and psychological effects. Therefore the words of St. John, "But if we acknowledge our sins, then God who is faithful and just will forgive our sins and purify us from everything that is wrong" (1 Jn. 1:9), bring us the message that may save us not only hours, but even years of misery and pain. However, not all pain is due to hatred, worry, or fear, there may be other causes. Nor does sin express itself only in physical pain. It may later be expressed in psychological problems, or in a crippled personality, unless we confess it to God and receive full release from it. Thus, forgiveness of sin, through direct confession to God, is a great privilege for the Christian.

But God goes even further than that, for we may commit sin that we do not recognize as evil; yet, it is sin, and the effects are the same upon the person. God offers to set us free, even from the unknown sin, if we walk honestly before Him. Sacred Scripture says, "But if we live our lives in the light, as he is in the light, we are in union [communion] with one another, and the blood of Jesus, his Son, purifies us from all sin" (1 Jn. 1:7). Thus, we need only to walk openly and honestly before God, confessing our every *known* sin, and He will forgive us also for every *unknown* sin. Therefore, the Christian has an advantage over all others to be free from sin and all its effects.

However, we must acknowledge that some sins that are confessed, even with much sincerity, sometimes are not forgiven. In fact, we may ask, "Have you ever confessed a sin more than once?" Some confess the same sin over and over again for years, thereby indicating they have not received forgiveness. How can that be if God has promised forgiveness upon confession, and we have confessed so honestly? It is because we receive God's blessings through faith. If, however, we have committed a sin that we simply cannot believe God can forgive, or we are so laden with guilt and fear that we cannot reach out in faith, then we do not receive forgiveness. Does this mean that in the really deeply entrenched need God disappoints us? No, quite the contrary. As Saint Paul says, "When law came, it was to multiply the opportunities of falling, but however great the number of sins committed, grace was even greater" (Rom. 5:20). But we must believe that God can and does forgive.

Many of us have ignored the New Testament teachings of confession to God. Some have emphasized the direct confession to God, but, by ignoring confession before others, they have driven many people who should have had their help from those in the Body of Christ to the non-Christian psychiatrist, psychologist, and counselor. We should not blame those that are seeking to help when we ourselves do not give help.

Three positive statements of Jesus that are relevant to confession, that many have neglected, are recorded in the Gospel. In Matthew 16:19, Jesus says to St. Peter, "I will give you the keys of the kingdom of heaven: whatever you bind on earth shall be considered bound in heaven; whatever you loose on earth shall be considered loosed in heaven." Later, speaking of our relationship to one another in the church, He says again, "I tell you solemnly, whatever you bind on earth shall be considered bound in heaven; whatever you loose on earth shall be considered loosed in heaven" (Mt. 18:18). We believe the context of the above passage, which speaks of the Lord's presence with two or three, but have ignored these words about binding and loosing.

Then after His resurrection: "And he said to them again, 'Peace be with you. As the Father sent me, so am I sending you.' After saying this he breathed on them and said: 'Receive the Holy Spirit' " (Jn. 20:21-22). He gave them this authority, "For those whose sins you forgive, they are forgiven; for those whose sins you retain, they are retained" (Jn. 20:23). We must recognize that these are tremendous words of power and authority to the Church, far too great to be ignored or misused. Yet, many have ignored these words of power to loose those that are bound and to declare forgiveness to those who cannot forgive themselves. So by the failure to exercise these words, we have left many in an unforgiven state and many bound to sins from which they should have been set free.

A very attractive, young woman had repeatedly suffered intense pain several days at a time for 15 years. Since no medicine would relieve it, I knew that it must be from another cause. However, she knew of no contributing cause and had come from a very happy home. As I prayed with her, I asked the Lord to enter into the events of her life surrounding the time when the pain began. I accepted, in faith, forgiveness for any sin that might have been committed, for she had confessed to God all that she knew to be sin. By faith in Christ, we broke the tensions, drove out the fears, and declared her to be free. She had been right in the midst of her pain, but within an hour it suddenly stopped. She wondered how long the peace would last, but I encouraged her to believe God concerning it. The next morning she came to tell me that God had shown her the cause of her problem. Although it was not a big sin in our estimation, it was so wrapped in fear and guilt that though she had confessed it many times, she had not been able to trust God for forgiveness. She had finally dropped it from her conscious memory, but it was not forgotten by her unconscious, and there it caused the pain. All she needed was the help of someone who could, in faith, declare God's forgiveness to her. When we then placed before God the whole problem that was brought back to her memory and accepted God's complete forgiveness, her release was tremendous. (It proved that there remained some other factors related to her pain, but her release was complete, and for 25 years we have kept in touch and observed her great freedom.) We can well imagine the great release when finally the unconscious has been told that it can "let go" after 15 years of holding onto guilt. Often, though the cause of the problem is not brought back to memory, its effects are completely removed by the word of forgiveness.

Therefore, we need to hear that word of absolution that can set us free.

Many have questioned whether such authority has been given to mankind, yet they have exercised those words of forgiveness in their personal witness for Christ and may only need to learn to apply them to other needs. Often when they have been helping people to come to Jesus Christ, they have encountered someone who has met all the conditions, and yet, does not feel that anything has happened. At that point they have said, "On the basis of God's Word you are forgiven; you are a child of God." This is the same word that can be said to the believer who has sinned and has confessed his sins before someone who is able to believe and declare forgiveness. Confession, of course, does not need to be within a "confessional." In the confession, we acknowledge our sins to God before man. The one hearing the confession takes the authority that Jesus has given and declares the sins to be forgiven. In reality, only God can forgive sins. However, we can declare, in faith, forgiveness wherever God has offered it when the conditions of true repentance, and confession, and authority are met.

In the context of inner healing, and leaving, for the moment, the question of public confession for public sins, we can say that the criteria of whether confession needs only to be made directly to God, or whether it need also be made before man, seems to rest on whether one has been able to believe God for forgiveness and so receive it. If forgiveness has been received, there is no need to make confession again. On the other hand, the one who is fit to hear confession and declare forgiveness is the one who is able to believe that God forgives sin on the basis of His Word, and who is able to exercise the authority that Jesus has given through the Holy Spirit. For it is the Holy Spirit who makes the authority of Jesus real in us. We recall that Jesus preceded His words about declaring forgiveness with the command, "Receive the Holy Spirit. For those whose sins you forgive, they are forgiven; for those whose sins you retain, they are retained" (Jn. 20:22b-23). Thus, the believer who has received the Holy Spirit has been given the authority to effect forgiveness.

The declaring of forgiveness is twofold: spiritually, it is taking the authority that is committed to the believer by Jesus Christ; psychologically, it is a word spoken to the unconscious of the one making a confession. He may consciously know that God is forgiving him, but inwardly he cannot believe it. This word, spoken by the believer, and with the authority of God, reaches the unconscious, and from there he takes hold of it. Only afterward may he realize that it has taken effect in his life, and he knows that he is forgiven and has no need of confessing that sin again. This is what makes the heart rejoice and praise God. It may be that a boy or girl in school will acknowledge to a friend, and to no one else, a troubled condition over a sin that he or she has confessed to God many times, but for which he or she has not received forgiveness. This friend, if he can believe God, may then declare that forgiveness, and it will be recognized in Heaven and in his friend's soul, for "whatever you loose on earth shall be considered loosed in heaven."

The healing of memories goes even further than the forgiveness of sins that we have committed. Many hurts come to people that are not any fault of their own, such as the death of a mother at an early age, the strife in a family home, or the rejection of a child by his mother before he is born. These traumatic experiences leave marks upon the unconscious and are sometimes expressed in obsessive fears. Fear is a warning of danger, as pain is a signal of organic trouble; and therefore, both are necessary. However, if a fear persists, something is wrong. Christ has come to set us free from fear. "In love there can be no fear, but fear is driven out by perfect love: because to fear is to expect punishment, and anyone who is afraid is still imperfect in love" (1 Jn. 4:18).

Sometimes, as a result of past experiences, one will be under tension for years, or be bound or stunted in emotional development, or be held under a great depression from which he cannot free himself. His struggle only makes him sink deeper. He needs the strong hand of another to lift him out of his condition. This is the power and authority that Jesus gave to us to set others free.

Sometimes inner problems are manifested outwardly in physical conditions. A responsible leader was unable to ride in a plane without airsickness after he had been in two near air crashes. It was easy to see that the memories of those times of great fear upset his stomach when he stepped into a plane. His work, however, demanded much flying, so we asked the Lord to heal the memories of those past experiences. When shortly afterward he flew across the Pacific, he told how happy he was to fly again without becoming airsick.

Another physical symptom of an inward problem was given by a woman as she shyly asked if we might pray about the chewing of her fingernails. She said that since childhood she had been embarrassed to show her fingers because of that habit, and yet it was more than a habit. Chewing her fingernails was only an evidence of that which was gnawing at her inwardly. She did not know the cause. So, we just asked Jesus to relieve her inner frustrations as a child, or at the time when this need began to express itself in chewing her fingernails. She also had a weight problem with which the doctor could not help her. Two weeks later, she delightedly showed us her fingernails, which had now begun to grow normally. She had also lost ten pounds. If the problem is related to areas of need for which Jesus died on the cross, we should expect that faith in Him and His finished work will meet that need.

Many people are tied up emotionally, and no amount of prayer and dedication has set them free. A Christian businessman told how he could not express himself to people. His wife told me that she could never tell how her husband felt about things with which they were concerned. As we talked, I asked if he came from a happy home. I find it no longer relevant to ask whether one has come from a Christian home, for too many so-called Christian homes are not happy homes. They are filled with tension, worry, resentment, and fear. This man had come from a home where the parents fought continually, and he had lived in fear. He had been afraid to express himself as a child and had been bound up emotionally ever since. It was this child within him, as a man, that was still bound and kept him from expressing himself to his wife and business associates.

Based on what I learned from Agnes Sanford, the wife of the late Rev. Edgar Sanford, who some years ago received the concept of healing of memories, I asked that Jesus go back in time and take that little boy on His lap and let him know that he was loved and accepted. I believed that Jesus was healing his hurts and making him know that he could express himself freely as a little child and that his fear of people was being taken away. Jesus did just that, for a few days later he told of having attended a meeting in which he had expressed himself in a way that he could not have done previously.

The rejection of a person can cause very deep and lasting hurts, but as we have been accepted in Jesus, these hurts can be healed too. A doctor in Thailand took me to see a leper patient. The leprosy was under control, so that was not the immediate concern of the doctor. This woman had been rejected by her village, her friends, and her husband and family, and the doctor was afraid that they would lose her even though the leprosy was under control. It was for this the doctor wanted prayer. She was a Thai woman and knew no English. I knew no Thai; so we could not communicate. But the doctor, who held her hand as I prayed in English, noted that each time I asked God for the healing of the rejection, this woman responded physically. Even though she could not understand a word that was said, her unconscious understood and responded. However, the real evidence came as healing began to take place. This had to be followed up by further healing of other memories, for God can do through us only as much as our faith will allow. We sometimes say that God can do anything, but that is not the question. The question really is—What can God do through us? How great is our faith in the abundant provision made for us on the cross?

We stand amazed at the deep needs that God meets through our prayer of faith. We know that this work is of God and not of man, and that we are only channels of His power. Yet, we know also from experience that only as we believe God in practical experience for that which we have long believed in doctrine or theory are these great needs met.

While we were in another country, a man called to ask if his wife, who had been subject to depression for several years, could come in to see me. We were able to spend only an hour together. In clinical counseling, to reach the level of such a need as this may take many months, or even years; then once identified, there is a possibility of healing. However, such time was not available to us. We prayed for the healing of memories, and she wrote the following a few days later:

"For several days after seeing you, I was still plagued with a constant headache that had persisted for several weeks. Then, quite without reason, the headache lifted last Wednesday. Since then, I've experienced a wonderful change within, and have at last been at peace with myself, my family, and with God. It is as though a great burden has been lifted, leaving me free to unbend and relax. Surely, the experience is a miracle—I thank you both for your faith and prayers. God has surely been with us and is blessing us so much. Even in the few brief days out of the depression, I have been through several events that normally would have thrown me into a deeper depression. However, as each has occurred, I have been able to deal with it on the spot, without bottling things up. I believe that it is a sure sign that God has answered your prayers. Normally I crumble under any stress. Today we received a letter from my mother. How I praise God for it. I am more than pleased to be able to sign off with love and mean it. All the hurt and unhappiness experienced when my parents disowned me has disappeared. In its place I have been filled with a new, deeper love for my parents. At Easter time we hope to drive back to—. It was there that I was so bitterly disillusioned by the church—but again, when I think about those who were responsible, the bitterness and hurt is no longer there. Surely, God is good."

Obtaining this kind of release demands our complete forgiveness of all who have wronged us. Jesus said, "For if you forgive others the wrongs they have done, your heavenly Father will also forgive you; but if you do not forgive others, then the wrongs you have done will not be forgiven by your Father" (Mt. 6:14-15, NEB). Does that mean that God is like the pouting child that says, "If you do not forgive, then I will not forgive you?" No, this principle of forgiveness is a law written into God's universe. As we have already seen, if we hold on to resentment, then physical illness or other problems may come to us. We cannot be released ourselves, if we do not release others. I often ask, however, "Are you willing to forgive?" instead of "Have you forgiven?" for I often find there has been an attempt made to forgive, but the attempt has been unsuccessful. And yet, if there is a willingness, God will make the ability to forgive possible as we accept that in faith also.

When a person is under deep depression, counseling may be impossible. Then simple questions may be sufficient. "Were you happy as a child?" If the answer is "Yes," then ask, "When did you become unhappy?" For depression is evidence of unhappiness. Then, perhaps, "Why did you become unhappy?" These questions are asked to pinpoint the problem for our help in prayer. Since depression is often suppressed anger, forgiveness is also a way of lifting depression. However, I have often prayed for the healing of memories without knowing anything more than that there was a need, and yet God did a great work.

In November of 1974, I was invited to speak to a small home group sponsored by an Anglican priest and a Mennonite pastor in Bancroft, Ontario. I was told that there would be people asking for prayer afterward, and my attention was called particularily to Brenda because she had suffered much in psychiatric hospitals and was in great need of help. After the lecture on dreams that long evening, with many people having questions and several coming for prayer, Brenda also came.

As we had done with many others, Lillie and I asked the Lord Jesus to go back into her past, even to the womb, to heal the hurts that were there. We accepted God's promise for her and thanked Him in advance leaving it there without seeing any evidence of change and going on to the next appointment the next day. However this is what Brenda told us later:

> "Somehow I floated out of that room. I had no idea of what had happened, but I knew I had never felt like that before...I was just bubbling...I couldn't sleep when I did get home, just lay there enjoying the way I felt. I think it was about three weeks before my feet began to touch solid ground at all."

I knew nothing of this until I received a letter from Brenda four months later. When she had shared her experience with her psychiatrist, he was utterly amazed at what had happened in his patient and asked for her prayer. Then I learned that she had spent 16 years under psychiatric care in many hospitals and received the largest dose of LSD given at that time; she had been given at least 50 shock treatments and even a partial lobotomy. It was no wonder that the doctor was amazed at her healing.

Brenda was now able to drive her car to Toronto for advanced schooling. She graduated from the Toronto Bible

College, studied Greek and Hebrew at Wycliffe College, the Anglican school of training, became an Anglican priest and later a chaplain at the General Hospital in St. John, New Brunswick. In these 26 years she has never again suffered from the depression of those early years. This does not denegrate the work that her fine psychiatrist had done, but it is evidence that there are areas of healing that can only be touched by the Spirit of God.

It is for the encouragement of faith, both in us and in the one for whom we are praying, that we try, if possible, to know more about the needs. But as we shall see later, the Holy Spirit is faithful to guide us in prayer, so that a common remark after prayer is, "How did you know to pray for that?" We do not know unless the Holy Spirit guides us, often beyond what the person himself can tell us.

It is so much better if we deal with the problems of children while they are little. A kindergarten teacher, after learning about the possibility of prayer for small children, found experiences in this area very worthwhile. One little five-year-old girl had serious emotional problems. Her mother had been in an accident one and a half years before the child entered kindergarten, but even before that, she had not been a good mother. Little Sandy was continually running to her teacher for affection: "Several times during the period of two and one-half hours," her teacher recounted, "she hugged me, sat on my lap, and expressed a desire to live with me. Also, she had a persistent tummy ache." The teacher continued, "I offered a very short prayer for the healing of her memories. Later, she said she still remembered our 'little secret' (of prayer), but since that time (except for the day after the prayer), she has not mentioned the tummy ache, nor does she come to me constantly for affection."

A prayer like this for children may even be made silently, as long as it is in faith. Sometimes, it may be best to pray for the healing of memories for little children when they are asleep, so that no suggestion regarding the cause of their problem, of which they may now be unaware, will be picked up by them consciously and be burdensome to them. Adults, when they can, need to enter into the spoken prayer consciously, and join in the faith of the one who is leading the prayer; but with little children, we can begin to pray before they even understand.

We know that children who are not wanted by their mothers, or are being carried while their mothers are filled with fear, anxiety, and hatred, will have problems in later life. Even before they are born, they are marked for trouble. How thankful we can be that God's healing also reaches back before birth! And how wonderful it is that some, without the psychological training that others have, can quickly learn to believe God for the healing of memories.

I had prayed for such healing for a man from another country. I was told that he was greatly changed, and that he immediately began to apply his newly experienced insights. He prayed for a young couple for whom the Lord did great things. They immediately responded in faith and prayed for their little one-year-old boy, whom they had adopted when he was two days old. Did he remember the events leading up to his adoption? Consciously, he did not, but unconsciously he remembered all, and the unconscious memory had already begun to express itself in his actions. However, the parents prayed for the healing of the hurts that he had received in the loss of his mother and in the events that preceded this loss. Even others noticed the change in that little boy, in his response to his parents.

Perhaps every adopted child needs prayer for the healing of memories. We thank God for the love of the parents that have received the child, but that may not be sufficient to heal his past hurts. Whether these past hurts include the loss of the mother through death, or the rejection of the child by his mother (and all the anxious thoughts that lead to such rejection), these traumatic experiences all need to be healed. A hospital chaplain in Australia said that even prayer for the healing of the child's memories was not sufficient in one case. She had prayed for this, but the child continued to show the same symptoms. Then she and his legal parents were led to pray for the child's natural mother, asking God to enable her to release the child, whereupon healing took place. We need to continually listen and learn how God's great power may be trusted for the complete freedom of each person.

The ones who are to exercise this great ministry of setting people free must know the power and authority of the Holy Spirit. This is not done by man's wisdom, but by the power of God. Without the power of the Holy Spirit, we cannot bind or loose with the authority that heaven will recognize. We may say the words, but they will be powerless. It is evident, also, that one's life must be clean by repentance, confession, and forgiveness offered to all others. This does not mean that our lives must be perfect, or that we must wait for years to elapse before we begin. It simply means that our lives must be free from all known sins and in tune with God.

It is important that we listen. First, we must listen to God to see whether He wants to use us for a particular need. A need alone does not constitute the call to its ministry.

We must know that the Spirit is directing us to minister to this need. However, let us not be deceived by thinking that if we do not hear the voice of the Lord in a certain way, then we should not minister. First of all, we know that Jesus has given us the command and authority to set the captive free. Therefore, we come to God with a positive approach, asking the Lord to check us if we are not to proceed. He will take away our peace or not give us full freedom if this is not our task, and we must then stop and ask for further direction. But if we feel the freedom to proceed, then we need to do so boldly, even though we may, at times, through our giving way to our own desires, or the pressures of the need, misunderstand or misinterpret God's direction. Nevertheless, it is better to make a mistake in learning to listen than not to listen at all.

Once we know that God wants us to meet a certain need, then we must proceed with three levels of listening. We must listen to what the person says concerning his need. We must listen to what he really means, for so often secondary needs are mentioned, but the real one is buried under shame, or fear of exposure. Then we must listen to what the Holy Spirit says to us, for He may tell us to pray for something that we have not yet heard from the needy one. Therefore, we must be very sensitive both to the people and to God. Sometimes we pray silently for needs that the Spirit mentions to us, but we do not feel free to mention this to the one for whom we are praying.

It is also absolutely imperative that we believe God if we are to exercise His authority. We must be persuaded inwardly that words Jesus spoke are meant for us, and that He will do what He has promised. An intellectual assent to the statements is not enough. It is said that it takes the unconscious three times as long to "catch on" as the conscious, but until faith comes from the heart, we do not yet have real faith. We must believe that, as we are praying, Jesus is *at that very moment* doing the things we are asking for, namely, breaking the tensions, lifting the burdens, driving out the fears, and healing the hurts, so that at the close of the prayer we can say, "Thank you. It is done." If we cannot thank God that it is done, then the prayer is of no value, and we would have been better off not to pray. But if we act in obedience to the leading of the Spirit, and pray in faith that we are being heard, then God will most marvelously manifest His power, and we will see the work done.

Let us remember that much greater things may yet happen through the prayer of faith than have here been mentioned. By this prayer, for instance, the homosexuals have been completely and permanently delivered. How quickly the Church has condemned such people, being totally unable to help them, yet saying at the same time that Christ can save us from all sin. It is we that stand condemned if, while condemning these people who want help, we remain unable to help them. Many such people have been led innocently by others into the trap from which they cannot free themselves.

We need to invite Jesus to go back into people's lives as they confess their sins, and ask God to make them know His complete forgiveness; to change the pattern of their lives; and to enable them to find their fulfillment in proper creative expressions. We need to free others from the bondage they have come into through the possessiveness of their mothers or from the fears they have known through the cruelty of their fathers. Often, it is fear, resulting from a seemingly insignificant experience, that follows a person all through his life, threatening to spring upon him at the slightest provocation. These things need not be so, for Jesus Himself says, "So if the Son makes you free, you will be free indeed" (Jn. 8:36).

It may be that one prayer will reach a level that is sufficient for the moment, but that further prayer will be needed at a later time. We can do only as much as our faith will reach. Furthermore, the depth that is reached at a certain level of prayer may be all that a person can stand at a certain time. Later, that person will have to be set free in other areas. There is much work to be done when one has begun to be set free, for he must guard that freedom, and he must allow for growth.

It is important, after we have asked God to set people free from past bondages or to heal them from hurts, that we ask the Holy Spirit to fill these areas of their lives, for they must not be left empty. Here, also, we must seek the Lord's direction, since we must not ask that one be filled with power unless the person is prepared for it; he may just need the healing, comforting presence of the Holy Spirit and His inner strength before he is prepared to serve others.

For others, the healing of memories is the necessary preparation for the empowering of the Holy Spirit. A psychiatrist told us that when he learns of a patient's early problems through hypnosis, he must be careful that he does not reveal to the patient more than that for which he or she is prepared. However, we have a great advantage here, for if we have learned to listen to the voice of the Spirit of God, we can be sure that He will not tell us to do anything for which the needy person is not prepared.

There is no doubt that there is a greater power in this ministry than that which psychology or psychiatry can offer, for sometimes problems that would take two or three years of counseling to uncover are not only uncovered but healed within an hour through prayer. But here we must be very careful, for we may have much to learn from the psychologist about men and women's problems to better be able to help them through prayer. Yet, it is evident that God must have a better way than years of counseling to meet the need of people who cannot afford the cost of such counseling, or whose need is too urgent to wait years for help. Let us not presume, but rather be humble and learn all that we can. Jesus said in His first sermon, "Blessed are the poor in spirit," or "How blest are those who know they are poor," for the poor are ready to receive from anyone. When people are ready to learn the truth from *whatever* source it may come, then they will be rich indeed, for "the kingdom of Heaven is theirs." (See Matthew 5:3.)

There is another way that the healing of memories may take place, for God has many ways to do His work. All the works He prescribes to us are works of faith, and I have found that some of our sacred practices have lost their power because they have lost that vital relationship with Christ through faith. So it was with baptism. As important as it is, it often has little effect upon the lives of many who receive it. This should not be so, and it is not so if it is exercised in the faith of the power of God. After I had seen the power of God set people free from all their past by declaring forgiveness and release, then I could see the relationship of the healing of memories to baptism.

In Colossians 2:11-12, St. Paul says, "In him you have been circumcised, with a circumcision not performed by human hand, but by the complete stripping of your body of flesh. This is circumcision according to Christ. You have been buried with him, when you were baptized; and by baptism, too, you have been raised up with him through your belief in the power of God who raised him from the dead." Therefore, in baptism, we are being set free from the sins of the flesh, for it is a spiritual and not a physical circumcision.

How does this take place? It takes place "through your faith in the active power of God." This evidently is the faith not only of the one being baptized, but of the one that is doing the baptizing. In that act of baptism that Christ ordained for the Church, the old life is cut off and the new person is set free to live out his new life. It is like ground that we prepare for a garden. We do not throw the seed among the weeds, but we pull out the weeds first, so the new seed will have a chance to grow. We know that weeds will grow again, but we pull out all the former weeds, so the new seed can get a head start. So, as the one who baptizes believes in the active power of God, he, in faith, pulls out all the weeds of the old life, so the new life has a proper chance to grow.

A young man, for whom the missionaries had great hopes of his becoming a national pastor, was brought to me. He had completed his training for the ministry but had completely failed in his personal life. I listened to him for two hours as he told me about his home, his past religion, his mistakes, sorrows, and fears. He was carrying a great burden, yet he was expected to become a successful Christian leader and to help set others free. He had been baptized, but not in the faith that God was cutting off all the past, and so he was still carrying it. He would have been freed from the burden if his baptism had been carried out with faith in the active power of God to cut off all the old life. This was not the young man's case; instead, he was still in bondage to his past. Therefore, I took the authority God has given us and set him free by the authority of binding and loosing.

What a new beginning it would be for many if after they had received Jesus Christ as Savior, they would be set free from all the past, and would then be ready to receive the Holy Spirit in fullness! That is why St. Peter could tell the sinners they should repent, believe, and be baptized, and they would receive the Holy Spirit. There need be no waiting for the believer to be taught and to mature before he is baptized; but he can be baptized immediately after receiving Jesus Christ into his life, and if the baptism is carried out in the faith that the power of God is cutting off the old life. When that is done, then the believer is also ready to receive the Holy Spirit in power.

What a change could be brought about in the church if every believer were set free from all past bondages, hurts, and fears. They could then know that they are forgiven indeed and could accept themselves, knowing that they are accepted by God. But in order for this to happen, there must be mature believers in the Church who, in the authority of the Lord Jesus Christ, can declare forgiveness and set the captives free. Then the Church will be able to begin to minister to the needy, and will not have to send them apologetically to the world for whatever help they can get.

I, myself, found that once I was set free from the fear that held me, I could begin to grow in an area of life that was bound since childhood. What a release it was to realize that part of my personality was suddenly freed! But now, I needed a mirror to see myself, so that I could allow my personality to come into balance. To my amazement, I found that God had already given me that; I only needed to learn to use it. And I must share this realization and development with others, so that they, too, may believe and develop to maturity and claim the authority that enables us to set others free.

Questions for Discussion

1. What is the scriptural basis for inner healing?
2. Who can declare forgiveness or absolution for another person's sin? On what conditions?
3. What kind of conditions require inner healing?

Chapter 3

How God Speaks to Us

It is surprising to many in this generation that the men and women of the Bible heard God speak to them. Yet from the beginning, in the Garden of Eden, we read that God and man spoke with each other. It is quite common to read the prophets' phrases "The Lord says" or "The word of the Lord came to me" before a proclamation, and to read at the close of their message from God, "I, the Lord, have spoken it." And Jesus took it for granted that His followers would recognize His voice. In speaking of the shepherd, He says, "...the sheep follow because they know his voice. They never follow a stranger but run away from him: they do not recognize the voice of strangers" (John 10:4-5). Then He says, "I am the good shepherd; I know my own and my own know me. ... The sheep that belong to me listen to my voice; I know them and they follow me" (Jn. 10:14,27). So it is apparent that we are expected to hear and recognize the voice of God.

God speaks, and He expects us to understand and obey Him. However, He speaks in many different ways. He spoke to people of the Bible through a voice, a vision, a dream, a conversation, an angel, a word of prophecy, or even by taking them up to heaven for a special revelation. But we have ignored many of these forms of communication. Morton Kelsey has summarized the reason for this in his earlier writings.[1] Plato stated that there are three valid sources of knowledge. The first source is the five senses, which we share with the animal world. The second is reason, which sets us above other creatures. The third Plato called "Divine madness," by which he meant the whole spiritual world of God and satan, angels and demons, dreams and visions, and prayer and spiritual communication. However, it is said that Aristotle, Plato's student, changed this concept, and first introduced the rationalistic philosophy of the Western world. It is understood that he eliminated Plato's "Divine madness" as a valid source of knowledge; that is, he denied the whole intuitive faculty by which divine perception comes to man; thus, the five senses and reason remain as the only valid sources of knowledge. Much of the Western world has been influenced by that thought. In Eastern and primitive cultures lacking this Aristotelian bias, the spiritual world of dreams, visions, and supernatural beings, is a common topic of conversation in the marketplace. In the modern West, it has become only the secret language of the Christian, and therefore, must be defended when referred to in the business world. We do not speak freely of our communication with the spirit world.

---

1. Morton Kelsey, *Tongue Speaking* (New York, NY: Crossroads, 1981).

In Western culture, we have been robbed, stripped, beaten, and left half dead—like the man in Jesus' parable (see Lk. 10:30)—by materialistic philosophy. We say that we are Christian, and we have founded our faith on the teachings of the Bible; yet, there are great portions of the Scriptures that we count as irrelevant for today, and we give to them only historical value. We may wonder why in the past God spoke to people through dreams and visions and angels but does not today. We may be shocked to realize that He has been trying, usually in vain, to do so in this day, but we have had our ears firmly shut to any voice coming from such a source. With this background, let us approach Scripture to see how God spoke to His people.

It was apparently by an inner voice that Abraham heard God tell him to leave his country, but the voice was clear and persistent enough so that he obeyed it. Elijah called it the "still, small voice." However, Jeremiah said that the word of the Lord to him was like fire in his bones that could not be contained. God spoke to Moses, first, out of the burning bush, but later face to face. The ways in which God spoke to these men were varied and perhaps seldom audible to the physical ear, but these men entertained no doubt that they had heard the voice of God through the inner ear of the heart.

The prophets had such definite communication with God that they sometimes had heated discussions with Him. Follow the line of conversation in Jeremiah 15:15,18-19 (TLB):

Then Jeremiah replied, "Lord, you know it is for your sake that I am suffering. They are persecuting me because I have proclaimed your word to them... Yet you have failed me in a time of need! You have let them keep right

> *on with all their persecutions... Your help is as uncertain*
> *as a seasonal mountain brook–sometimes a flood, some-*
> *times as dry as a bone." The Lord replied: "Stop this fool-*
> *ishness and talk some sense! Only if you return to trusting*
> *me will I let you continue as my spokesman. You are to in-*
> *fluence **them**, not let them influence **you**!"*

These men were not shy about speaking to God and dis-
cussing their problems with Him. God even drew up a con-
tract with Abraham, that was valid between Abraham's
descendants and God for centuries afterward (see Gen. 17).

On occasion God sent an angel to bring His word to
His people. Abraham was about to carry out a drastic act
of obedience to God when the voice of an angel stopped
him and gave him other instructions (see Gen. 22). The
mighty angel Gabriel was sent to Daniel, as he was praying
for Israel and the nations (see Dan. 9), and to Mary as she
was to become the mother of Jesus (see Lk. 1). It was
through an angel that God's orders were carried out to set
Peter free, in answer to the prayers of the church (see Acts
12). It was also an angel that stood beside Paul in the
storm (see Acts 27). We should not think it strange, then,
that God may, at this time, send an angel when He has a
special message for us.

There were also those who were caught up to heaven
and heard many revelations from God, even of things
about which they were forbidden to tell, as the apostles
John and Paul record. Strange as it may seem to us, these
are all ways that God spoke to people long ago. And He
still speaks to us in these same ways today.

In the book entitled *Vanya*, the author relates that in
1971, an angel came to the Russian soldier Ivan as he was

being persecuted for Christ's sake.[2] One night, the angel came and took Ivan up through the ceiling and roof and on into another world. While Ivan was gone, the man in the bunk beside him searched the room but could not find him. Ivan's faith had been so tested that this was the encouragement he needed to continue his stand for the Lord.

Inasmuch as Jesus expects us to know His voice, it follows that the very first step toward that recognition is to get to know the Lord Jesus Christ personally. Receiving Him into our innermost being is not a superficial act, but rather a deep experience of the heart so that "...anyone who is joined to the Lord is one spirit with him" (1 Cor. 6:17). His Spirit, then, relates to our spirit in the deep unconscious part of our personality. "Everyone moved by the Spirit is a son of God. The spirit you received is not the spirit of slaves bringing fear into your lives again; it is the spirit of sons, and it makes us cry out, 'Abba, Father!' The Spirit himself and our spirit bear united witness that we are children of God" (Rom. 8:14-16).

God is continually speaking to us. Most commonly, He speaks to us through the Scriptures. They are the word of the Lord to us; they give to us the general principles of obedience for all occasions. In the Bible, we can find those principles that we need to solve our problems. Jesus said, "If you remain in me and my words remain in you, you may ask what you will and you shall get it" (Jn. 15:7). We need to live by the Word of God and feed from it upon Christ daily. If we fill our hearts and minds with the Word

---

2. Myrna Grant, *Vanya* (Altemont Springs, FL: Creation House, 1974), 62-65.

of God, we will understand the ways of God, and as we do so, we will receive the general direction for our lives.

But if we are to receive specific direction concerning our daily walk, such as getting a job, buying a house, or other matters on which the Bible does not speak in detail, we must learn to recognize the voice of the Holy Spirit. We read the Bible, which is a "lamp to my feet, a light on my path" (Ps. 119:105), but to understand it we must have the illumination of the Spirit of God. Jesus said, "But when the Spirit of truth comes he will lead you to the complete truth… " (Jn. 16:13). St. Paul wrote, "The Spirit reaches the depths of everything, even the depths of God. After all, the depths of a man can only be known by his own spirit, not by any other man, and in the same way the depths of God can only be known by the Spirit of God" (1 Cor. 2:10b-11).

The Lord guides us in many ways, all of which require listening and discernment. He may speak to us through the events of daily life—the state of bodily health, the people who come to us, the surprises that happen, the words that we hear during the day, what we receive from the Lord in sermons, in sharing with friends, or when we are alone with God. This is a language that requires delicacy in interpretation and not the arrogance of our notions imposed upon it.

According to the promise of Jesus, we have, in this day, the direct guidance of the Holy Spirit (see Jn. 14:16). The mysterious voice of this spiritual friend, unknown to the unbelieving world, becomes the familiar voice of God to those who walk with Him. However, even among Christians, a question is repeatedly raised concerning how to recognize the voice of God. We know that He speaks to us today by His Holy Spirit, but we do not recognize His voice. There are many voices that speak to us: our own desires, public opinion, the pressures of authority, and satan's deceitful voice of temptation, pride or presumption. Out of all these voices, and more, how shall we sort out the voice of God? Furthermore, how can we be so sure of His voice that we can make important decisions of life based on that recognition?

Recognition of the Holy Spirit's voice is like the recognition of the voice of a loved one. The unique imprint of that voice was made when we first heard it, and then through further contacts we learned to recognize it. The voice of God's Spirit was also imprinted upon us when we became children of God, and as we obeyed it, we came to recognize it. However, many of us have since lost that initial recognition through the rationalistic philosophy of this world that denies any kind of communication with God. Thus, we doubted, then failed to obey, then became confused, and now hardly think it is possible for anyone to know the voice of God.

As the Holy Spirit is continually speaking to us, we need to ask Him to teach us again to know that voice we first heard when we received Jesus Christ into our lives. When He speaks to us, the Holy Spirit may bring a Scripture portion to mind, a circumstance of life, a thought, an impression, and often a mental picture or vision. To receive the word of the Lord through any of these avenues, we must chart our course carefully between two dangers. Our most imminent danger is that we will receive nothing from God unless it comes in a prescribed way—a way with which we have become familiar. However, we must realize that God speaks in many ways, and He has acquainted us with these ways in Scripture. The other danger is that we take every word, thought, impression, or picture as from the Lord, forgetting that many things can come from our own feelings or thoughts, or even from the enemy. Therefore, it is necessary to ask from God and trust Him for His protection over our minds and spirits while we wait silently upon Him.

When we hear a word from the Lord, we must trust God concerning it, just as a little child taking her first step trusts her father. When Sally takes that step and promptly falls, her father does not scold her; instead, he is so delighted that he announces happily to his wife that Sally is learning to walk. God is our Father. He is as delighted as any parent could be when His child learns to walk in His ways. Therefore, we need not be afraid to commit our way to Him, but begin to act in obedience to that which we believe is the voice of God giving us guidance. If we make a mistake in listening to the wrong voice, God will graciously pick us up, overrule our mistake, and correct our understanding, as long as in our hearts we honestly want to hear and do the will of God (see Ps. 37:23-24). Thus, we learn, even through our mistakes, and when we listen correctly, we have the joy of having heard the Lord and receiving the answer to our request. Gradually, *through obedience,* we will learn to differentiate between the voice of God and all other voices. Thus, we may listen privately, with two or three others, or even in a larger group.

If a group waits silently upon the Lord in this way, the members must be willing to share whatever they receive, and also be willing to have every word or impression tested by the group. When there exists such an openness before the Lord, God is faithful to confirm that which is from Him by giving several people the same message, often in completely different ways. The listeners must also be willing to disregard those things that are not confirmed. Herein lies the safety of a group.

At a time of crisis, my wife and I visited a disciplined group to ask for prayer. I was told that it would be better if I did not tell them the nature of our need. They began to wait upon the Lord. They prayed, some read Scripture with which they were impressed at the time, and others remained silent. Then, one received a vision but did not know what it meant. Soon another began to interpret the vision and others added to it with Scripture or word until we knew clearly what we should do. However, that prayer group did not know what our situation was until we told them at the end of the waiting period. Then, we all rejoiced together, for the Lord had clearly shown us in a supernatural way what to do in our dilemma. Afterward, the members of the prayer group stressed for us the importance of each one's part. One received a vision, another an interpretation, another a word of Scripture. One received nothing at all, but was depended upon completely for confirmation concerning what was said to the others. If there was not complete unanimity in the group, they would stop immediately and check to see if they were hearing correctly. We will see later in this chapter how all guidance must be tested, for we are dealing with a realm unfamiliar to us. We are operating in a realm where satan can gain entrance if we are not exceedingly careful, but it is, at the same time, the sphere in which God has always moved to commune with His people. He will guide us if we walk humbly and carefully before Him.

Although God speaks to His children by His Holy Spirit, there is another way in which He speaks to all people alike, believers or unbelievers. It is a language most of us have ignored, and therefore, needs many pages devoted to it. It is not more important than other ways in which God speaks, but as it is less understood, it needs more explanation. It is the universal language of the unconscious, namely, the language of dreams and visions, through which God provides a counselor for people to understand themselves. The dream is, also, a mirror in which we can see the reflection of our inner selves daily. It is a voice from within that speaks in every person. There is no educational requirement to understand it, for it speaks in the simplest language; yet, its depth reaches beyond the understanding of the best psychiatry. Though it is universal, and much reference is made to its counsel in the Bible, most of us have ignored its message. But it is the nightly messenger. God has spoken through dreams and visions, from time immemorial, to people of all races, but we in the West have been too sophisticated to listen. We have disregarded this voice because it comes through such strange means of communication.

Here science comes to our aid to remind us that God's Word is relevant for all times, even in the strange communication through dreams and visions. In recent years, many studies of sleep and dreaming have been made in such leading universities as New York, Chicago, Cornell, Duke, McGill, and many others. Some significant facts have come to us through these sources. We are told that every person dreams an average of at least one hour per night. Through many tests, it has been discovered that dreams are essential to people's physical and mental health, and when one makes up sleep, he must also make up dream time. Through the use of the electroencephalograph, it can now be determined just when in sleep the dreams take place. A less sophisticated method is to watch the sleeper's rapid eye movements (REM) and observe that, during dream time, his eyes will move under his eyelids, as though watching a picture. After observing the eyes of one such dreamer, researchers asked him whether he was watching a tennis match. The dreamer replied: "No, I was watching my neighbors toss tomatoes back and forth over the fence." So the eyes do actually take part in the observation of the dream. We are told that a person can be driven to a point of insanity by continually being awakened during dream time, which is not the same as being awakened at other sleep time. In the economy of God, it would only seem logical that if God made the dream to be so important to people's physical and mental health, it would also have something to say to us.

Psychology comes to aid us further in this research. In fact, I believe psychology has found its place of importance because it has been the means of reminding us of truth that the Church has long neglected. Sigmund Freud, though a materialist, showed incontrovertibly that dreams had something significant to say to man. Carl G. Jung, working with Freud in this research, came to the conclusion that the message of the dream came from a far wider base than sexual repression. Dr. Jung estimated that in his lifetime he interpreted some 80,000 dreams of people from many cultures all around the world. From these studies, he discovered that the dream compensates for imbalances between the conscious and the unconscious, or the outer and inner parts of the personality. He too contended that the dream has something to say, and it is up to the dreamer to get the message that the dream is carrying from the unconscious.

But the dream speaks in symbolic, not rational, language and must be so interpreted. We have almost lost the use of symbolic imagery. This may be why we find the dreams and visions of Daniel and Ezekiel and the Revelation of Saint John so hard to understand. However, there remains vestiges of symbolic expression in our day to day lives. If a political cartoon shows an eagle and a bear fighting, we do not interpret it rationally, as a study in biology, but as symbolically referring to the countries represented being in conflict.

Jung also pointed out how personal every dream is. There is no fixed interpretation for each symbol, but each dream relates strictly to the dreamer's life. On the other hand, many symbols are drawn from figures familiar to all people through the ages. We will see how all these things are illustrated in the dreams, visions, and interpretations of the Bible, for that is our final authority.

I was amazed to learn how much the Bible had to say about dreams and visions. From earliest time, Elihu gives counsel to Job:

In saying so, I tell you, you are wrong: God does not fit man's measure. Why do you rail at him for not replying to you, word for word? God speaks first in one way, and then in another, but not one notices. He speaks by dreams, and visions that come in the night, when slumber comes on mankind, and men are all asleep in bed. Then it is he whispers in the ear of man, or may frighten him with fearful sights, to turn him away from evildoing, and make an end of his pride; to save his soul from the pit and his life from the pathway to Sheol. With suffering, too, he corrects man on his sickbed, when his bones keep trembling with palsy; when his whole self is revolted by food, and his appetite spurns dainties (Job 33:12-20).

The principle spoken of here, so long ago, is very true to the experience of life today. God may speak to people in three ways. First, He may speak with the inner voice. If they do not listen, then He may speak through the dream and may "frighten (them) with fearful sights." And if people do not listen to the dream, God may put them on a bed of pain.

Now let us see how God spoke to the people of the Bible. From the earliest records of the patriarchs, the strong impression is left that these great people believed God actually spoke to them through dreams and visions. God called Abraham to leave his home and country, and Abraham obeyed. When he questioned God about his heirs, God showed him the stars and then spoke to him through a vision (see Gen. 15). But Abraham still wanted confirmation of God's word, for his test was great. This time God showed his future through a dream, and gave him the great Abrahamic covenant. God told him that his descendants would be exiles in another land. This gave him encouragement to live as a nomad instead of settling down and building a city, which his descendants later would have to leave.

Jacob is no example of ethics in his early life; nevertheless, God, through a dream, encouraged him through the beautiful picture of the ladder with the angels going up and down on it, and promising him His care (see Gen. 28). Jacob remembered this dream when his own ways came to a sad end and he needed such a word to help him. Gideon was fearful, but was encouraged by hearing the dream of a soldier of the enemy forces, who understood what it meant (see Judg. 7). So the language of the dream is universal to believer and unbeliever alike.

We can easily see how Joseph's dreams were so personal and so literally fulfilled (see Gen. 37). The images of the dream were taken right out of his everyday experiences—the sheaves, stars, sun, and moon. The brothers' belief that God spoke in dreams is evident by their anger that their younger brother should have such a revelation from God. How many times these dreams must have come back to Joseph in those discouraging times in jail. A picture impresses itself upon the mind even more than words, and thus, the dream is not easily forgotten. He must have believed that God spoke through dreams, in spite of the fact that his own dreams did not seem to be any nearer to fulfillment when he interpreted the dreams of the butler and the baker (see Gen. 40). Again, the imagery comes right out of the common scenes of the lives of the dreamers; even the numbers in the dream are significant to the interpretation. The butler's dream showed that his service would in three days (represented by the three branches) come to life again (represented by the budding, blossoming, and the bearing of fruit of the vine), and he would again serve Pharaoh. This must have encouraged the baker, who evidently did not recognize the picture of the birds eating from the tray as being similar to vultures eating carion, and so picturing his death. But as the dreams indicated, so they were fulfilled. Therefore, Joseph's earlier dreams must have given him an appreciation and understanding of dreams that was later used by God.

It is gracious of God to show the future to such a man as Pharaoh (see Gen. 41). But if we dreamed his dreams today, we would be apt to say: "What a ridiculous dream—seven lean cows eating seven fat cows, and seven thin ears of corn eating seven fat ones." That is so only because we try to interpret dreams rationally. What could be a better picture of the prosperous seven good years being devoured by the seven years of drought? The shift of interpretation from rational to symbolic makes all the difference. Joseph's explanation of why the dream came twice is helpful to the one who asks why he has repeated dreams. The message is important, and God is trying to get through to him. Fortunately, Pharaoh heeded the message of the dream and saved his land.

In First Kings, chapter 3, we are told how Solomon made a transaction with God. In a dream, God gave Solomon the opportunity to ask for whatever he liked. In the dream, Solomon asked for an understanding heart to lead God's people. Still in the dream, God tells Solomon he asked wisely, and so He offers him riches and glory as well. Did Solomon say when he awakened, "What a strange dream I had" and forget it? No, he accepted God's message to him and celebrated the gift God had given by giving a public banquet. How differently we treat God's message that comes to us through dreams.

The messages of the prophets are filled with dreams and visions. This is according to God's word to Miriam and Aaron when they complained, "Is Moses the only one with whom the Lord has spoken? Has He not spoken with us as well?" God heard them and said: "...If any man among you is a prophet, I make myself known to him in a vision, I speak to him in a dream" (Num. 12:6). This is exactly what God does with the prophets. Take note of the great dreams of Daniel and the visions of Isaiah, Jeremiah, Ezekiel, Joel, Amos, Obadiah, Micah, Nahum, Habakkuk, Zechariah, and St. John the apostle. Thus, according to the word that God spoke to Aaron and Miriam: "If any man

61

among you is a prophet I make myself known to him in a vision, I speak to him in a dream."

Both Scripture and psychology agree that the dream and vision are the same; only the vision is given to us while we are awake, the dream comes while we are asleep. God comes to Jeremiah the prophet and says, "What do you see?" God calls the dream and vision dark speeches or riddles (see Num. 12:6-8). The dream is God's elementary language to all people. Some think they can skip the elementary lessons and speak to God as Moses did; and yet, they have difficulty recognizing even the voice of God.

Daniel's dreams are personal, as were Joseph's, but Daniel is already involved with the nations; therefore, the dream is not only about him but about the nation Israel and the other nations related to her. Our dreams seem to be as big as our interests are. As Daniel's experience is so much bigger than the average, so the dream also includes his larger interests.

Carl Jung once had a dream in which he saw all Europe laid out before him in a bath of blood, except for a few islands that protruded. He did not understand the dream then, but after the Second World War, he recognized that the islands he saw in the dream were those countries of Europe that had not been involved in the war. God had given him a picture of the future, which surely included him but went far beyond. Undoubtedly, those dreams are given that we may do something about the situation, or that we may prepare ourselves for it. God, in recent days, has been showing through visions and dreams the future of individuals or churches who seek Him.

Some, however, will say that this may be so for the days of the Old Testament, but we are living today and there is little said in the New Testament about dreams and visions.

On the contrary, it is amazing to see how many important events of Scripture hinge on dreams and visions. The moment that we step into the New Testament records, we are astounded at the utter confidence that people had in the message that came through the dream.

Let us put into a modern setting the first experience with a dream in the New Testament. Suppose your son's hope has been shattered because his fiancé has evidently become pregnant. Suddenly he comes to you thrilled and excited, saying that God has shown him, through a dream, that the young woman's pregnancy was a supernatural intervention of God, as she had said, and she had not been with another man. We would probably ask the young man who he was trying to fool. It would take more than a dream to make us do what Joseph did. (See Matthew 1.) Yet, on the message of one dream, he took Mary to be his wife, risking all the misunderstanding that would go with it. He evidently believed that God not only spoke through dreams, but that He spoke the truth and the dream's message was to be relied on. Yet, we have no indication that his dream was any more real than ours. It was on that basis also that he followed specific guidance for the safety of his family. He was told through dreams, and he obeyed the message received—to move to the strange country of Egypt, when to return, and where to live. Undoubtedly, we need a restoration of faith in dreams as a vehicle of the message of God, in order to receive guidance from Him.

There are more records of visions in the New Testament than of dreams; and yet, we are even less likely to believe their message. It was through a vision that the angel Gabriel came to Zecharias and told him that his wife was to have a child (see Lk. 1). If Zecharias was disciplined with nine months of silence because of his unbelief, then our discipline must be even greater. By means of visions, the followers of Jesus saw the angels after His resurrection, and we know that Jesus appeared in this way to Paul for his encouragement (see Lk. 24:23; Acts 18:9). It is our rationalization that has blinded us to such possibilities.

A woman, who had told a pastor that she had seen a vision of Jesus and that He had spoken to her, received as his rationalistic reply that it could not have been Jesus that appeared to her, for no one had ever seen Him and so the likeness could not have been His. We need only remember that Jesus and the angels often appeared in a recognizable form. A woman, well known to us, was sitting at her sewing machine in sorrow weeping when Jesus appeared to her in a vision. Not a word was spoken, yet the loving, compassionate look on His face has been a source of great comfort and encouragement to her ever since.

Visions, like dreams, may come to all sorts of people. Sometimes they appear like a single scene, sometimes as a television picture before the eyes. As attention is paid to these pictures, which are far more common than we might have thought, they have proved to be meaningful, pictorial messages brought forth from the unconscious for the occasion, for God speaks through the unconscious.

The transfiguration, which Jesus calls a vision, may provide some explanation of this strange phenomenon. We can imagine that as Jesus was deeply moved about His coming rejection and death, He took three of His closest companions with Him to pray. Suddenly, as He prayed, the glory of God came upon Him, and Moses and Elijah appeared talking to Him. Perhaps Moses and Elijah had already come to Him, but only through the vision were the others able to see them. This experience may have been similar to that of Elisha's servant who was afraid when he saw the armies of the enemy surround their little town (see 2 Kings 6). When Elisha prayed that the servant's eyes would be opened, he saw the hills covered with horses and chariots of fire. Evidently, the spiritual army was already there, but he could not see it until his eyes were opened, and then he had better vision which enabled him to see into the spiritual realm. Thus, we may ask, "Is the vision simply the removal of the veil from our eyes, so that we can see really or symbolically what is already there?"

Jesus' experience on the mountain, in the time of great trial, encourages us to believe that God can show us more of reality through a vision than we can see with our natural eyes.

Some may still hold out and say that now that we have the Holy Spirit, we do not need dreams and visions. However, the promise of the coming of the Holy Spirit is linked with just these elementary means of communication. Peter, quoting from the prophet Joel, says: "In the days to come—it is the Lord who speaks—I will pour out my spirit on all mankind. Their sons and daughters shall prophesy, your young men shall see visions, your old men shall dream dreams" (Acts 2:17). The coming of the Holy Spirit upon the Church today has not diminished, but increased, the use of dreams and visions. We need to find the relationship of the Holy Spirit to dreams and visions, as we shall see in the next example.

The vision and dream has often been the means of solving difficult problems. Dr. Austin Hale, with the Summer Institute of Linguistics and member of the faculty of the University of Kathmandu, Nepal, said that as a student, he worked hard on his mathematics problems and got his answers in his dreams, a perfectly valid method, and now often gets help for his linguistic problems in the same way.

God used a vision to get the Church to solve the universal problem of integration. But to solve that problem, He had to remove a big prejudice, as is so often the case. Peter had heard that the disciples were to go to the Gentiles, for Jesus reminded them of that after His resurrection. But for the Jews to accept the cursed Gentiles into the same church that they had come into by the Spirit was too much, even for Peter. Then God gave him a vision by which he saw himself and his prejudice. In true symbolic fashion, Peter saw the sheet let down from heaven with all kinds of animals in it. He was told to kill and eat, but he said that as a Jew he had never eaten anything unclean. Then came the significant word so often succinctly given in dreams. In this case, it was, "What God has made clean, you have no right to call profane" (Acts 10:15b). This was the point of the vision, but he did not understand what it meant. Then the Holy Spirit told him where to go, and in the middle of his sermon in a Gentile home, he suddenly understood what the vision meant. This is the usual way that the understanding of dreams and visions comes, not by study or rationalization, but by sudden realization. He had called the Gentile unclean, refusing his entrance into the Church, and the vision revealed his prejudice.

Dreams and visions do not spare us, but show us clearly what we are inwardly. They are the best natural counselors that we can find, and they can help us solve the most difficult problems if we are willing to face the truths they carry to us.

As if all that dreams and visions have said is not enough, we find that the New Testament ends with 22 chapters of pure visions concerning the future, based upon the dynamics that are at work in history. The dream, like the vision, is able to tell about the future, even in the non-believer's life, because it draws from a source that is deeper than his own conscious or unconscious experience. It seems to borrow from the collective unconscious of all humanity. A friend dreamed of the death of a loved one in another country. She paid no attention to it until the following afternoon when she received a telegram of this one's death. This is not by chance, but is a feature of the dream that is often not realized.

The dream and vision sometimes predict the future, often not as absolute, but as a warning following God's law relating to prophecy (see Jer. 18). If the warning of the dream is heeded, then the judgment predicted does not need to take place; if not, then it is fulfilled, as told in the dream. So it is, also, concerning the encouraging message of the vision or dream. It does not take place automatically. If the one receiving the message heeds the word with faith and obedience, then the prediction will be fulfilled; if not, then it was only a promise that one has failed to realize. This we often see in the messages of the prophets.

If God gives so much direction, reproof, and help through dreams, then it is evident that we should listen to them. But you may say that you do not dream. In this, you are contradicted by the research of today, indicating that we all dream, every night, unless our dreams are inhibited, possibly by some drug or alcohol. Some say that they only dream when they eat heavily, but it is more likely that heavy eating makes us more restless so that we awaken during the dream and remember it. Then why do we not remember dreams? It is because we have trained ourselves to regard the dreams as ridiculous nonsense to be forgotten. As soon as a person pays attention to dreams, he begins to remember them, but even then, they are often lost the first few minutes after awakening. If we are persuaded that God speaks through the dream, then we will consider it worthwhile to have pencil and paper conveniently placed so that some facts of the dream can be written down, even while we are still awakening. If we write down a few notes, then the rest of the dream can be more easily recalled later. But the whole dream must be written out just as it is, without any changes, for the details are significant. If after repeated attempts we cannot recall any dream, we may need to ask ourselves whether we are shutting out some word that we do not want to hear.

It is advantageous to relate the message of the dream to our devotional time with God. The dream shows us what we are like inwardly, and where we are going. Then in our devotions we can ask God for help or correction, or we can give Him praise. A man dreamed that he was delightfully swimming down a stream with some large porpoises. The same night, he dreamed that he was in a big passenger boat that was taking him in the wrong direction, and he felt as if he was being deceived. The first dream encouraged him in giving expression to his new creative drives, for he was in the midst of a new project. But the second told him to beware of public opinion, represented by the passenger boat, for it would lead him in the wrong direction. The Scriptures so often confirm our guidance or shows us the way to find help, for both the Scriptures and the dreams are from God.

But you may say that if God and His angels can come to us through dreams and visions, then cannot satan and his demons do the same?

Nowhere in the Bible are we warned to be careful of our dreams. The only warnings are to be careful of the false prophets who have consulted idols or mediums, for they will have false or imitation dreams or visions. God said to Zechariah, "For the idols have spoken vanity, and the diviners have seen a lie, and have told false dreams; they comfort in vain" (Zech. 10:2a, KJV).

Dreams, therefore, are safe for all people, whether they are believers or even unbelievers, like Pharoah and Nebuchadnezzar. It is only if people consult mediums, or go to seances, that they may get false dreams or visions, or imitations. Unfortunately, people who have given themselves over to witchcraft and evil forces are being deceived by satan. Otherwise, all dreams are safe instruments of God.[3]

Are all dreams of equal importance? No, not any more than all thoughts are of equal importance. Some are called "big dreams," for they may give a grand picture of our lives for years ahead. Some may be corrective, some instructive, some may be great and contain symbols of special significance that can be understood only through prayer, or through the help of those more experienced. It is important to have the help of a trusted friend with whom we can discuss our dreams because it is hard for us to be objective and keep a balance. All visions and dreams given to a group need the testing of that group.

---

3. Herman Riffel, *Dream Interpretation: A Biblical Understanding* (Shippensburg, PA: Destiny Image, 1993).

The seemingly insignificant and foolish dream may have an important message. When we write down the dream, we will usually be tempted to think there is nothing to it; but it is only as we see the whole picture, and listen, that we understand. Even the details are significant. It is important to know whether you were in the basement or the upper floor of the house in your dream, for the basement may speak of your dealing on the level of the lower instincts, the upper floor may speak of your mind.

But the big question is, "How can I understand my dreams?" The first step is to be quiet and listen, and ask God to show you what it means, for He gave it to you. Don't expect the answer to be some great and mighty revelation. The dream often speaks very simply and revealingly but symbolically, that is, by a picture language. Therefore, we must put our rational thinking aside and ask what the picture represents.

A woman came to seek help in her relationship with her husband. She was honest and said that she often did not have the patience to wait and so interrupted him, even in conversation. When she told her dream, it was this: She was riding a motorcycle in heavy traffic and was trying to pass the other cars by constantly cutting in, until she almost caused an accident. It was not difficult for her to see, in this graphic picture, what she was doing and what would happen if she continued in this way. The dream had used the language of pictures and symbols after speaking to her, more directly, through the inner voice. The emotion-filled dreams of falling may indicate that we are not on solid ground psychologically. A boy dreamed that he was tied to a railroad track and the train was coming. This revealed an inner condition of frustration of which others did not seem to be aware. In these ways, God gives us warnings, and tells us to do something about our situation; for danger is near. It is no wonder that some people "go to pieces" when they ignore God's warnings. If we are driving a car in the dream, it may mean that we are in control of the situation; but if we are a passenger in a car that is going where we do not want to go, it may indicate that we are not in control of ourselves psychologically and are being "taken for a ride." Thus, dreams use the simple pictures of outer life to reveal important conditions of our inner life.

To find the meaning of the dream, we can also ask ourselves how we feel about situations in it. If we are not properly clothed before others in a dream, we must ask ourselves what we are uneasy or embarrassed about in life. This is what the dream reflects of our inner person, for that is just what we would feel like in real life, if we were not properly clothed before others. We may be flying without the use of a plane, which may suggest that we are "flying high" psychologically and are not in close enough touch with reality.

The birth of a child may represent the birth of a new idea or concept. If you follow this "child" in the dreams, though it may be represented by different children, you may see it grow from infancy to maturity over a period of years in the dream, as the idea grows in real life. One man, strongly taken with his new concept, saw it first as a baby in a carriage that he drove right over the house, illustrating the way that the new idea overcame all obstacles. The baby grew in the progressive dreams to manhood. At one point, he dreamed that he was on a swimming dock with a ten-year-old girl for whom he was responsible. Suddenly, she fell into the water, and he was just able to grab her by the heel and pull her out. He awakened quite shaken. As he stopped to listen, he realized that he had not paid attention to his "idea," and it was pictured as almost being lost into the unconscious. He paid careful attention to the concept that God was developing within him, and it grew to maturity, both in his real life and in his dreams.

One man said, "I dreamed that I was attending a funeral service, but I was also in the casket." The "I" attending the service was the ego, the conscious part of himself, for the ego is not the whole "I." The other, in the casket, was a part of himself that had died. Only the dreamer could know whether that was good or bad, though another may help him to understand what the dream could mean. The part of himself that had died could be a part that he had long tried to deal with or dispose of, or it may be a neglected part of himself that had finally died. We must pay careful attention to the warnings and reminders of the dream.

However, we may ask how we can know whether the dream is objective or subjective. This understanding comes from waiting and listening and learning. We are told that 95 percent of dreams are subjective, that is, when we dream of others the dream is speaking symbolically of ourselves. It shows us the many parts of our personality, the part that needs healing or creative expression, or the parts that are in conflict. First, it is best to approach the dream subjectively, for God is much more interested in telling us what to do, than our telling others what they should do.

Objective dreams are comparatively rare, though we hear of them most often. We must be very careful how we handle them. We, as Christians, have the great advantage of the Holy Spirit's help, but it seems many have not even learned to listen to the unconscious through which the Holy Spirit speaks.

The dream is very personal, as we have seen in the dreams of Scripture, and it reflects the response of the inner man to our outer, conscious actions. So, when we dream about people, we are usually dreaming about ourselves, and it has nothing to do with the other person at all. When a man dreamed of a very dogmatic friend, knowing he was not that type of person, he wondered why he should dream of him. He stopped to listen and recognized that, just at that time, he was dogmatically defending a certain position. The dream was an up-to-date reflection of his inner thinking and, thus, gave him opportunity to correct his actions. Thus, when we dream about another person, we must ask what this person represents to us or what he reminds us of, and what we are doing in real life that he is doing in the dream. In this way, the dream is like a mirror of our soul.

Since our whole person is revealed in our dreams, the animals in our dreams play a vital part, for they often portray animal instincts in us. It may be necessary to study carefully the habits of animals, so that we can better understand their part in dreams. One who is being attacked by large and powerful animals that attack head-on, such as the bull or the elephant, may need to take control of his emotions, as they are about to overwhelm him. If he begins to deal with those emotions, he will find that the animals in the dream may change to the cat family. As in nature, the cat does not charge head on, but attacks from behind, so also, the dreamer can observe that he is no longer threatened to be overwhelmed, but is nonetheless being attacked from behind. As he continues to deal with his emotions and desires, he may see only a mouse gnawing in his house in the dream, thus indicating that his problem is almost solved, but there is still a little gnawing desire that needs to be taken care of. The dream is always related to our life situation, and a dream without information concerning the dreamer's present state is of little value.

Birds also may appear in the dream, and their meaning will depend on the type of bird. Is it a vulture, representing the kingdom of darkness, or is it a dove from the Kingdom of light and peace?

In the dream, we can also see the neglected part of ourselves that needs expression. This may be depicted by fear of someone who is chasing us. As in real life, to get rid of the fear we must face it. A nightmare is the same as a dream, only filled with fear. Therefore, we must face the man or animal that is chasing us in the dream and ask who it is. A mother said she prayed that her children's nightmares would be taken away. This is like asking that we do not hear the fire alarm. We should, rather, ask that God would take away the cause of the fear that is turning the dream into a nightmare. It is so good to deal naturally with children. One mother said it was the custom when she was a child to have dreams as the frequent breakfast conversation, and now, as a mother, she continues the same with her children. We can deal very simply with the dream and very gently with the child. What is the general impression of the dream? If it is fear, then we may well ask what the child is afraid of, and we may discover deep, hidden fears that the child has not been able to verbalize, but the dream has pictured. If it is joy, then we can be encouraged. This can be a happy adventure, solving problems before they get too large, and enlarging the child's capacities for imagination. The reading of C.S. Lewis' Narnian books for children may well accompany such an experience.

But let us remember that we may be just beginners in learning the strange language of the dream. It takes years to learn a language, therefore, as we learn, let us "play it lightly" and let us not press for the interpretation. Let us be willing to listen to our dreams, even if we get only a few helpful suggestions at first. In our western civilization, we are generally out of balance because we have almost completely neglected the unconscious and put all our efforts into conscious actions and decisions; thus, we have been robbed of our inner insight and power. On the other hand, primitive people are often out of balance because they have highly developed their unconscious powers and can speak for hours of their dreams, but they have greatly neglected their conscious mental development.

As we learn to listen to God, we shall see ourselves. Daniel told Nebuchadnezzar that the dream was given to him so that he could "understand [his] inmost thoughts" (Dan. 2:30). The dream shows us that there are many secret thoughts and motives in our inner hearts that must be dealt with. If we refuse to bring into consciousness these thoughts of our innermost being and deal with them, we can expect the unconscious to respond with physical and psychological problems. Elihu warned Job about the danger of failing to listen to God. He suggested that if people do not listen to the word, then God may speak in a dream; and if they failed to listen to the dream, then perhaps "man learns his lesson on a bed of pain" (Job 33:18). It is so easy, and yet, so hard to really listen.

Similarly, God may want to show us things that concern our future, or the future of the people we serve, by visions that come from God and must be interpreted by the Spirit of God. If we learn to listen to the elementary language of the dream, we will be in a far better position to understand the higher visions that God has for His saints.

But all guidance from God, whether it comes through the inner voice, dreams, visions, angels, or by the Holy Spirit within us, must be tested. Even though the great men of God learned to hear the voice of God so that they performed great works for Him, they were not always sure of their guidance. Moses was a prophet par excellence, yet in anger he changed very slightly the direction God had given him, and was, therefore, set aside from bringing Israel into the promised land (see Num. 20:1-12). The prophet Nathan at first told David to go ahead with his plans to build the temple, for God was with him. But that night, the Lord corrected the word of the prophet (see 2 Sam. 7). Jeremiah thought he heard God's message of direction, but was not sure it was from the Lord until it was verified (see Jer. 32:6-8). The Holy Spirit said "No" to the great apostle Paul as he tried to enter certain lands, and then guided him through a vision to yet another country (see Acts 16:6-10). If these men of God needed to verify their guidance from God, how much more do we, who are just beginning to learn?

Guidance from God can be tested in several ways. If we "hear" or "see" something that does not agree with the teachings of Scripture, then we can know that it was not the voice of God, for God does not contradict himself. He will not say one thing in His written Word and then contradict that in personal guidance. The Scriptures always become the test for our personal word from the Lord. Of course, we know that we do not always have the proper understanding of the Scriptures, and we may need to take a second look to see whether the Bible really says what we think it says. But in the last analysis, if there is conflict between what I "hear" and what I read in Scripture, then it is the teaching of Scripture that must be followed.

Another test is the spirit in which a word is given. If it is a word of wisdom, then it must be in agreement with the attitude of the heart that James describes (see Jas. 3:13-18). "Whereas the wisdom that comes down from above is essentially something pure; it also makes for peace, and is kindly and considerate; it is full of compassion and shows itself by doing good; nor is there any trace of partiality or hypocrisy in it" (Jas. 3:17). But where jealousy and rivalry exist we find, as James tells us, wisdom that is earthly, animal, and devilish will express itself.

A third test lies in the peace that God will give us if we are in fellowship with Him. This peace is a very special gift that Jesus gives to His followers, "Peace I bequeath to you, my own peace I give you, a peace the world cannot give, this is my gift to you" (Jn. 14:27a). There is a false peace that a person may have if he continually denies the word of the Lord to himself, but that peace can be checked easily if he honestly seeks the Lord. The real peace of God cannot be imitated by satan.

Paul says, "...may the peace of Christ reign in your hearts... " (Col. 3:15). As long as we follow the leading of the Holy Spirit of God, He gives us His peace, but when we go out of His way, His peace leaves us. That is why the peace of God is to reign, or be the judge, or the referee (as some translations put it) in our hearts. By the presence or absence of the peace of God in our hearts, we can ascertain whether or not we are following correct guidance.

There is a fourth way by which we can confirm our guidance. The church, namely that portion of the Body of Christ to which we may relate, can be invaluable in affirming or evaluating our guidance. But this body can help us only as long as it is in unity and fellowship and obedience to the Word of God. The same Spirit that is in us is also in all other true believers. However, the Spirit can only guide a group when they are in harmony with one another and with God. When this is so, we may freely submit our guidance to our spiritual director, or another Christian, to see if he or she, too, recognizes it to be in accordance with the Scriptural principles, and has peace about it. Or, we may go to two or three others, or a larger group, with the same request. The Church is instructed to judge prophecy in this way (see 1 Cor. 14:29). The surety of personal guidance so often lies in the willingness of the individual to submit his guidance to the judgment of others in the church. When we face important decisions, we will want to have our guidance confirmed. God is quite willing to show us by a sign, as He did with Gideon, or through the confirmation of others, as long as we are willing to obey the guidance that He gives us.

It is a privilege to be part of God's creation, a creation with which God speaks, using, as He often does, the elementary language of visions and dreams. But what a great thing it is to have the Holy Spirit of God living in us to communicate with us. May we learn not only to speak to God, but first, to listen to Him, for He desires to speak to us. Then God will share His secrets with us, for He says, "The close secret of Yahweh belongs to them who fear him, his covenant also, to bring them knowledge" (Ps. 25:14). God could not hide from Abraham His plan to destroy Sodom and Gomorrah, for he had become a friend of God (see Gen. 18). We, likewise, will stand amazed at the things God has been waiting to tell us when we begin to listen to Him, and expect Him to speak in any way that He may choose.

Questions for Discussion

1. In what ways did God speak to the people of the Bible? How many of these ways do you recognize?

2. What great historical events, recorded in the Bible, came through dreams and visions?

3. What is the primary purpose of the dream?

4. How can we test whether the voice we hear is from God or from another source?

For further information on dreams, see the following Destiny Image Books:

Dreams: Wisdom Within, 1994;

Dream Interpretation, A Biblical Understanding, 1993;

Dreams: Giants and Geniuses in the Making, 1996;

and other excellent books for further study of dreams from the Christian perspective, like the following:

Morton Kelsey, *God, Dreams and Revelation*, Augsburg, 1991.

John Sanford, *Dreams God's Forgotten Language*, Lippincott.

Chapter 4

Man and His Power and Authority

As I faced the needs of the little boy with the brain tumor and the young man so desperately in need of release from bondage, I was forced to take another look at the Scriptures. Was it possible that the healings and miracles and signs that took place during the life and ministry of Jesus should still be occurring today? We had written them off as past historical events that were necessary to establish the Church; now that the Church was established and we had the Scriptures, they were no longer needed. But, I began to question that theory, for the needs *were* there, just as great as ever.

Then I began to wonder how Jesus performed those miracles. Was it by the power of His deity, or did He do them as part of humanity? I remember asking that question of my professor during my theological training. The answer I received was that we could not always tell when He worked through the power of His deity and when He lived as a man. But this question began to haunt me now. I knew that it lay at the foundation of my further ministry.

If Jesus did His miraculous works as God, then we could worship Him as God, but He was not an example to us, for we were part of humanity. But if He lived His life and did His works as one of human kind, then He was a great example to follow, a pattern of what we ought to be and do. The implications were great. Therefore I had to take another look at the doctrine of the humanity of Christ.

Here I found again how our doctrinal arguments confounded us. The defense of one doctrine has robbed us of spiritual power by causing us to lose sight of another. The evangelical church has spent much time defending the deity of Christ. There is no question that Jesus Christ was very God of very God manifested in the flesh; but in our eager defense of the doctrine of the deity of Jesus Christ, we have done serious damage to the doctrine of His humanity. Perhaps, we would have needed to write fewer words in defense of the doctrine of Christ's deity, if we had shown more evidence of His power in our humanity.

I am convinced that Jesus was limited completely to His humanity from the point of conception, when the life of God was implanted into Mary, until His death—i.e., He always lived and expressed Himself through His humanity. Let us consider this as we look at His life. His birth was like the birth of any other child. He was carried by His mother, and born helpless, having to be wrapped in swaddling clothes, all typical of the newborn infant. We know that He had to learn to walk, talk, read, and write as all the children of Nazareth did. Later, those of His hometown could not reconcile His teaching and miracles to what they had seen of Him, with His family, as He grew up in their village, for we read:

> *They were astonished and said, "Where did the man get this wisdom and these miraculous powers? This is the carpenter's son, surely? Is not his mother the woman called Mary, and his brothers James and Joseph and Simon and Jude? His sisters, too, are they not all here with us? So where did the man get it all?"* (Matthew 13:54b-56)

In view of His childhood, they had not expected Him to be different, for as a child, He evidently was just like their children.

"And Jesus increased in wisdom, in stature, and in favor with God and men" (Lk. 2:52), and as a boy of 12, He showed evidence of coming to Himself in a perfectly normal way for that age. When His parents took Him to the temple, He must have known that they would be worried about Him as He stayed away the first, the second, and perhaps even the third night, for He was a sensitive and obedient child. Why then did He do that? Was it not that He felt Himself at home in the temple, just as a boy who is a talented musician feels at home with his instrument? The child prodigy does not need to be told to practice, for that is the fulfillment of his driving force.

Evidently, Jesus felt at home in the temple because He found there the expression of His deep calling, as He said, "Did you not know that I must be busy with my Father's affairs?" (Lk. 2:49b) In one sense, He rebelled against His parents, for He obeyed something within Him that His parents did not understand. But He did not rebel because of a wicked heart, for He went home with His parents and was obedient to them in all other things. Jesus, there, became a pattern for all children who must separate themselves from their parents in order to become persons in their own right, in that which they know is their very own calling. In all other things, they are to do as Jesus did, who placed Himself under the authority of His parents.

We can get a better understanding of the great problems of His youth if we know that Jesus really was human. He must have heard the stories about His birth from His parents and become aware of His calling from them. But when His calling began to stir within Himself, and He began to pursue it, He would run into a great conflict. As He eagerly listened to the description of the Messiah from the Scriptures, He must have realized that the tradition about the coming of the Messiah that He heard in the village did not agree with the prophets. No doubt some of the questions that He asked in the temple caused amazement and left the teachers rather baffled. But this was only the beginning. The further He pursued the studies of the Scripture about the Messiah, the sharper would be the contrast to Jewish tradition. We can imagine that, as a young man, His discussion with the Jews of His day must have left Jesus much disturbed. He would see more and more clearly that if He followed the calling of God to be the Messiah, then He would run into direct conflict with the political powers of Israel. The choice to obey His calling must have had in it all the elements of our choice today to heed the Lord's call to whatever it might be, if we decide fully to obey.

Another clear indication of the humanity of Christ was His life of prayer. If we wonder whether prayer is human or divine, we only need to ask, "Does God pray?" To whom does He need to pray for anything? Yet, Jesus prayed continuously, in public and private, and in long hours of wrestling with God. He evidently drew upon the power of God through prayer, as we must do to remain strong in the Lord.

How difficult it must have been for Him as He knew that all the work that was to be done was to be done through Him in His humanity. His faith must have grown, as with us, for there seems to have been a progression of faith in His work, as in His raising of the dead. He first brought back to life the young man who had been dead only a few hours, whose body was in the casket on the way to burial. Then, in the face of much scoffing and unbelief, He brought back to life the little girl who had just died. Then, imagine how great must have been His struggle as Jesus received word that Lazarus was sick. Naturally, He would have wanted to heal him, but the Father, to whom He always submitted, said "No." He must have felt in His spirit that Lazarus had died, and yet, He was prevented from going there. As the time wore on, He knew that He would have to raise Lazarus from the dead by His own word. How He needed to hold on in prayer so that His faith would not falter, assuring the command to the dead man would not be powerless. He believed God for this, as we must believe Him. But how much greater was the struggle in prayer as He knew, by His perfect obedience, He would become the acceptable sacrifice for the atonement of the sins of the whole world if His faith did not fail. The temptation to give in so pressed in upon Him that:

> *During his life on earth, he offered up prayer and entreaty, aloud and in silent tears, to the one who had the power to save him out of death, and he submitted so humbly that*

his prayer was heard. Although he was Son, he learned to obey through suffering (Hebrews 5:7-8).

Therefore, Jesus' prayer life is the indication that, as a man, He wrestled with God as Jacob did long ago. How this makes us appreciate His humanity and His identification with us in our experience!

But as we consider the humanity of Christ, we must also consider His power by which He healed the sick, drove out evil spirits, and raised the dead. Prior to His baptism, He had performed no miracles (see Jn. 2:11). This is another indication that He lived out His life just as any person would, in perfect obedience to His Father. Then something happened that changed His life among people completely. When He was baptized in the Jordan, the Holy Spirit came upon Him, and there began to flow out from Him a series of miracles and wonders such as the people had never seen. This could be nothing else than the power of God. Yet, it was the power of God working through a man whom they knew well enough. But, they must have wondered how such power could come through a man. Some sought to know further, as Nicodemus did. Some became jealous and accused Him of using demonic power; but He warned them that this power was by the Holy Spirit, and it was not to be confused with satan's deceitful working.

This power worked in many miraculous ways to save and heal people. Jesus later told the disciples that they would receive such power when the Holy Spirit came upon them. And when that power came upon the disciples, they worked in the same way that Jesus did. The four Gospels and the Book of Acts, which contain over half of the New Testament, are filled with records of people working with such power.

Paul explains that the Holy Spirit manifests His power in many ways. Nine different abilities, or powers, are mentioned by Paul in First Corinthians 12, all of which were manifested in the life of the Church, and at least seven in the ministry of the Lord Jesus. They are called the gifts of wisdom, knowledge, faith, healing, miracles, prophecy, discerning of spirits, tongues, and interpretation of tongues (see 1 Cor. 12:8-10). In fact, if these gifts, and the results of their manifestations, were taken out of the Acts of the Apostles, all that would be left would be a good, dead, orthodox Church, if any Church at all. Furthermore, without these gifts of the Spirit, there would have been no power in the life of Jesus. He was called to save, not only by the power of a good life and by His death, but by the power that would heal the sick and raise the dead and deliver the oppressed from satan, that all might know that the Kingdom of God had come down to humankind (see Lk. 10:9), and have reason to believe in the Messiah.

I became persuaded that we have been so powerless because we have been afraid of the power that is made available to us. On a day in which I was desperately in need of power, I read from Acts 4:29, "And now Lord, take note of their threats and help your servants to proclaim your message with all boldness," and I asked again for that boldness, as I had done many times before. But then, I read the next verse, "By stretching out your hand to heal and to work miracles and marvels through the name of your holy servant Jesus" (Acts 4:30).

And I said, "Oh no, Lord, not this." I did not want to get involved in healing and signs and wonders.

But the Lord clearly said, "You want to be filled with the Spirit, do you not?"

"Oh yes," I said, "I have prayed for that many times. "

Then the Lord said, "But you want to be filled with the Spirit in your own way, so that when you preach many will be saved. However, the Holy Spirit works in many ways." This made me afraid, for there were some gifts that I did not want, even though I so needed power. The Lord taught me about boldness. What is the boldness of an attorney? Is it that he shouts loudly? No, he may calmly present his case, for he knows that he has the evidence, and that he can present that evidence at the right time and win the case. This was the boldness of the disciples. It was not a brashness, but a faith that trembled while it dared to mention the name of Jesus, upon which God produced the evidence. Peter may have been fearful of saying to the man who had been crippled for 40 years, "Stand up and walk," but he obeyed the voice of the Spirit, and God did the work.

This kind of boldness I could better understand, for I too could dare to name the name of Jesus, as long as God produced the evidence. But then I would have to allow the Spirit to work in the way that He wished. Earlier in my life, I was afraid that I might receive a spurious power that was not from God. But then the words of Jesus began to show me, "What father among you would hand his son a stone when he asked for bread? Or hand him a snake instead of a fish? Or hand him a scorpion if he asked for an egg? If you then, who are evil, know how to give your children what is good, how much more will the heavenly Father give the Holy Spirit to those who ask him!" (Lk. 11:11-13) Perfect trust in God takes away fear.

We imperfect Christians have built up still another reason to fear these gifts of the Spirit. We have left them in the dark; and what is in the dark, we are afraid of. Many of us have learned very little about the power of the Spirit by which Jesus and the Church did their works, because these gifts have remained in the closet of forbidden things. Therefore, let us bring them out into the light of God's Word and look at them one by one. We will find that there is nothing to be afraid of, though we may stand utterly amazed at them.

Some say that they will choose love, which is the fruit of the Spirit, rather than have anything to do with the strange gifts of the Spirit. We must remember that the choice is not ours. Jesus told the disciples not to leave Jerusalem until they were "clothed with the power from on high" (Lk. 24:49). We may compare the gifts of the Spirit to the tools by which a house is built, and the fruit of the Spirit, which is love, to the way those tools are to be handled. We use a hammer to build a house, even though we know that a hammer can be a dangerous instrument if it is not used with love. So a church that has the fruit of the Spirit without the gifts is like a husband who offers his wife love but is afraid to use the tools to build a house for her. Certainly the tools need to be used with love, but we do not pretend to use love instead of the tools. A church with the fruit, but without the gifts of the Spirit, may be a loving church but without power. On the other hand, a church with the gifts but without the fruit of the Spirit may be powerful, but may do much harm by the foolish exercise of the gifts. Therefore, we need to heed the injunction of the apostle Paul in First Corinthians 13, to exercise love along with every gift of the Spirit.

Paul points out the relationship of the fruit of the Spirit and the gifts in First Corinthians 13, for we must remember that the whole chapter speaks about both the fruit of the Spirit, which is love, and the gifts of the Spirit, which bring power. He begins by speaking about the gifts of tongues, prophecy, knowledge, and faith, and their relationship with love. Though we continuously take this beautiful chapter out of its setting, it is introduced and amplified by chapters 12 and 14, which are all about the gifts of the Spirit. Although it is a gem in any setting, surely we must not ignore this original context. Paul is here not talking about having love rather than the gifts, but having love with them. In fact, we may just as properly conclude from his words, that, "If I speak in tongues and have love, then I am not a sounding gong or a clanging symbol but rather a beautiful song or harmony. If I have faith strong enough to remove mountains, and have love, then I am not worth nothing, but rather a great deal." So it is not either love or the gifts of the Spirit, but it is the gifts with love that is to result in the power of the Holy Spirit.

But some will say that these gifts of the Spirit are not for today; they were given for the early Church, to establish it. That these gifts were given only to establish the early Church may be a rationalization to explain away our powerlessness, for we find this nowhere stated or suggested in the New Testament. When we study the Scriptures to find the line that we have drawn to determine which part of the New Testament is for today, and which is not, it becomes quite invisible. Paul does say that love is permanent, while these gifts are temporary.

*Love does not come to an end. But if there are gifts of proph-
ecy, the time will come when they must fail; or the gift of languages, it will not continue for ever; and knowledge—for
this, too, the time will come when it must fail. For our
knowledge is imperfect and our prophesying is imperfect;
but once perfection comes, all imperfect things will disap-
pear* (1 Corinthians 13:8-10).

But, then we must ask when imperfection ends and
perfection comes. "Now we are seeing a dim reflection in
a mirror; but then we shall be seeing face to face. The
knowledge that I have now is imperfect; but then I shall
know as fully as I am known" (1 Cor. 13:12). Have we
come to such perfection of knowledge that we know as
God knows? Certainly not, and that is the reason that we
need the gift of knowledge for our witness for Christ.
When we arrive at the place of wholeness, we will not need
healing, for there will be no sickness there; but now people
need to know the power of God to encourage them to believe. Jesus said, "But you will receive power when the
Holy Spirit comes upon you; and you will bear witness for
me in Jerusalem, and all over Judaea and Samaria, and
away to the ends of the earth" (Acts 1:8, NEB). When we
witness with this power, then all will know that the Kingdom of God has come down to earth, as they did when Jesus worked in the flesh.

God seems to be saying to us through the life of Jesus,
"See what a person can do if He will believe and obey Me!"
And Jesus is not only our example to follow. He walks before and beside us, but He is also in us. "Christ in us" is the
theme of Paul's Epistle to the Colossians: "In his body lives
the fullness of divinity, and in him you too find your own
fulfillment, in the one who is the head of every Sovereignty

and Power" (Col. 2:9-10). This is literally to be so in practice (not in theoretical doctrine only), so that when we lay our hands upon people in prayer, we can say in confidence that Jesus is laying His hands upon them through us.

What kinds of works should we then do? Jesus said,

> *In truth, in very truth I tell you, he who has faith in me will do what I am doing; and he will do greater things still because I am going to the Father. Indeed anything you ask in my name I will do, so that the Father may be glorified in the Son. If you ask anything in my name I will do it* (John 14:12-14, NEB).

So we are to do the same works that He did, for Jesus Christ has not changed, as the writer says, "Jesus Christ is the same today as he was yesterday and as he will be for ever" (Heb. 13:8).

The humanity of Christ, therefore, presents to us a challenge from which we cannot escape by the excuse that He was divine and we are not. It is as though God is saying, "Look what man can do if he will fully trust and obey Me." He came to live out His life in our flesh, first, to demonstrate how that life could be lived, and then to live it out through us. If we try to excuse ourselves by saying that it was different with Jesus, for He was not born in sin as we are—therefore, He had no sinful nature to contend with— then we must ask ourselves whether we really believe in the atonement. If God cleanses us from all sin when we confess it to Him, then we can also be free from all the past. The same Jesus that was born to Mary, and is also born in us, wants to live out His life through us by the power of the Holy Spirit and prayer. This is overwhelming, indeed, but it is the challenge left to us in the New Testament: the great hope for the world, as the Church demonstrates the power and authority given to it.

Maturity is necessary for people to be well and fully developed, but maturity is only the prerequisite for power. When a person has come to maturity, from a Christian point of view, he is responding to God with his whole body, soul, and spirit, and he is prepared to receive authority without misusing it. Jesus spoke with authority, and worked with power; and He gave this power and authority to His disciples. In contrast to the Church, we see described in the Acts of the Apostles, the Church of today has been not only an immature Church but a powerless Church. Therefore, we need to look at the Acts of the Apostles again, and see what power and authority they exercised, and which power enabled the early Church to turn the world upside down.

Questions for Discussion

1. What indications do you find in the life of Jesus revealing that He worked in His humanity throughout His lifetime?

2. What are the gifts or manifestations of the Holy Spirit? Where do you find them in the book of Acts? Where in your life?

3. What is the relationship of the fruit and the gifts of the Spirit?

Chapter 5

The Gifts of Wisdom, Knowledge, and Faith

The Church has not put much emphasis on the gifts of the Holy Spirit, but even so, these gifts are not altogether strange to us. Despite the fact that we have not identified them, we may yet have some practical familiarity with them. We have known of special wisdom given by God that solved a difficult problem. Or, we may have known of a mature Christian telling a younger man or woman, with some conviction, that he is called to a specific work. Perhaps, we were in the position of receiving such a word, and we saw it come to pass. Evidently, more mature Christians have always had the gift of knowledge, which the Church simply has not recognized as a gift of the Spirit. Or, perhaps, someone received a special faith that allowed God to do a great work, which later brought great praise to God. This may have been looked upon as an unusual work of God.

These all may have been gifts of the Holy Spirit that were not recognized as such by the Church. The twofold value of identifying these gifts is that Christians can then seek and expect that the gifts of the Holy Spirit will be given; and that when they are given, they will be recognized as gifts from God, and received with appropriate gratitude and thanks. We may also have wisdom as a gift for a time of trial. Jesus speaks of a wisdom especially given by the Holy Spirit for a time of crisis:

> *Remember, I am sending you out like sheep among wolves; so be cunning as serpents and yet as harmless as doves. Beware of men: they will hand you over to Sanhedrins and scourge you in their synagogues. You will be dragged before governors and kings for my sake, to bear witness before them and the pagans. But when they hand you over, do not worry about how to speak or what to say; what you are to say will be given to you when the time comes; because it is not you who will be speaking; the Spirit of your Father will be speaking in you* (Matthew 10:16-20).

So Jesus tells us that for a time of trial, we will not need to seek what to say, but words will be given to us.

We see this illustrated in the experience of Stephen, one of the seven chosen to help the widows in the early Church. He was qualified for the task because he was a man filled with the Spirit and with wisdom. However, God was going to give him a wisdom beyond that which he already had. As Stephen began to work miracles and signs by the Holy Spirit, he was challenged by members of the synagogue. Surprisingly, they found they "could not hold their own against the inspired wisdom" (Acts 6:10, NEB) demonstrated by this mere layman who had just entered the service of the Church. So, they gave full expression to the anger that arises in people who cannot answer an argument. They picked up stones to kill him. Jesus wonderfully fulfilled His word in this time of trial, for Stephen did not have to develop his own arguments but received words from the Holy Spirit. And so Stephen, gloriously entering the presence of Jesus, his Lord, demonstrated the Spirit's wisdom that cut unbelievers to the heart and the Spirit's love that offered them full forgiveness. That wisdom is a gift of God. (See James 3:15-18.)

Jesus Himself, in His earthly ministry, received the gift of wisdom in response to His perfect trust and obedience to God in His humanity. This was most apparent in His ministry in Jerusalem. The people were surprised that He was openly teaching others in the temple when it was known that the leaders wanted to put Him to death. The Pharisees and chief priests had sent officers to arrest Jesus, but they came back empty-handed with the reply, "No man ever spoke as this man speaks" (see Jn. 7:46). The words of Jesus had so impressed the temple officers, that they departed from Him in awe. Again, when He was arrested and on trial, He was given words of wisdom by the Spirit, which remain as a pattern for us today.

We may well accept these experiences in the life of Jesus, or Stephen in the early Church, but what about us in the commonplace circumstances of our lives? To illustrate, let me relate from personal experience what I later came to recognize as a gift of the Holy Spirit. It was at a time of crisis in my ministry, when my faith in the validity of the Scriptures was being challenged, that suddenly a new thing happened to me. I had learned 25 years earlier how to find the proper text, or subject, for the speaking appointments that would come three or four times per week.

I knew from experience that there can be a vital difference between a sermon and a message from God. A sermon may be just a compilation of chosen material, or it can be a message from God if the minister has sought the guidance of God for the occasion.

However, in this time of crisis, I received guidance neither for a Scripture text, nor for a sermon subject. It was a critical time and I became desperate, for I knew that my wisdom on the choice of sermon material for such a time would not be sufficient. Then the Lord reminded me of His instruction that when we are on trial, we are not to prepare our words, for He will give us words to say. It was with trembling that I went to the pulpit, not once or twice, but Sunday morning and evening for two months, not knowing what I was to speak about. Sometimes I did not know what to say until I actually stepped from the chair to the pulpit; and yet, afterward, I was told that I never had preached with such freedom and power as at that time.

Deep conviction of the Holy Spirit accompanied my ministry during those two months of crisis. I knew that this was beyond my past experience. The Holy Spirit had evidently given the gift of wisdom for the time of trial.

Shortly after that, I was to speak in another country to 200 Christian leaders who were well trained in their own fields. I knew that I was to speak twice per day for ten days on a subject that could be very controversial. Again the Lord gave me no freedom to prepare even one outline or to take any notes with me. But when I arrived, He gave me the words to say and great liberty and freedom in the presentation. Only after several years did I recognize that the Spirit, at that time, gave me an outline for presentation of this material. In fact, I gave that series of lectures 50 times in 16 countries.

I am continually amazed how well it has been received by many who are almost totaly unfamiliar with, and therefore fearful of, this important subject. So while I believe in the importance of preparation, I have concluded that the Lord would not allow me to prepare an outline or even a note for that conference because He had something special to give me for the future, as well as for those meetings. And all of this was related to my witness for Christ.

This same wisdom may come to a mother who does not know which way to turn at a critical point in the training of her children, or to a young man as he stands for his faith among unbelievers. When we remain faithful in our witness to Jesus Christ and trust in Him, then shall be fulfilled the words:

> *As scripture says: "I shall destroy the wisdom of the wise and bring to nothing all the learning of the learned. Where are the philosophers now? Where are the scribes?" Where are any of our thinkers today? Do you see now how God has shown up the foolishness of human wisdom? If it was God's wisdom that human wisdom should not know God, it was because God wanted to save those who have faith through the foolishness of the message that we preach. ... For God's foolishness is wiser than human wisdom and God's weakness is stronger than human strength* (1 Corinthians 1:19-21,25).

Similar to the gift of wisdom, but perhaps a bit more specific, is the gift of knowledge. I have found no specific identification of the gifts of wisdom, knowledge, or faith in the experiences of the New Testament believers, but rather illustrations of the exercise of these gifts as they worked under the power and direction of the Holy Spirit.

I believe we can see clearly that the gift of knowledge must have been given to Peter as he was leading that thrilling "testimony meeting" described in Acts 4:32–5:11, a meeting that turned into a terrible manifestation of the power of God. Barnabas had just brought the money from the sale of his estate and laid it at the apostles' feet. Now, Ananias apparently did the same. However, at that point, the apostle Peter evidently received a sudden insight into Ananias' deceit and challenged him with lying to God. What disruption and trouble that would have caused if God had not been in Peter's challenge! But Peter believed the word of knowledge, or insight, that he received from the Spirit, and spoke it under the direction of the Spirit. God immediately gave proof that the words of Peter were of Him by bringing the sudden deaths of Ananias and Sapphira. It was a terrible judgment, but through the apostles' obedience, and God's action, the Church's witness for Christ was preserved in truth. The result:

This made a profound impression on the whole Church and on all who heard it. ... No one else ever dared to join them, but the people were loud in their praise and the numbers of men and women who came to believe in the Lord increased steadily (Acts 5:11,13-14).

The gift of knowledge was given to help in the witness for Jesus, and in this strange and awful way, the witness to Jesus was increased.

Some may be very eager to receive the gifts of the Spirit, but may not realize that their challenge in the midst of a delightful fellowship meeting would not be popular. However, when the Spirit prompts us to use His gift, we must be obedient to Him. Therefore, let us first consider whether we are willing to exercise the gifts before we ask for them.

Under different circumstances, but with similar effect, we see this gift of the Spirit exercised in the life of Jesus on the occasion of His conversation with the Samaritan woman at Jacob's well (see Jn. 4). His witness was carried out in a masterful way as He turned His conversation with the woman from the discussion of natural water to the consideration of the living water. The woman then asked for the living water, and He asked her to get her husband. She replied that she had no husband. At that point, there might well have been a stalemate if the Spirit of God had not given Jesus the special gift of knowledge, or insight, into the woman's life. Remember, if Jesus was limited to human experience as we are, then He did not know all about the woman, but needed the help of the Holy Spirit as we do. When Jesus told her what the Spirit revealed to Him, she was in awe and said that he must be a prophet. She carried her witness to the village, saying, "He told me everything I ever did." The result was the same as in the apostle Peter's experience—many more came to believe in Jesus.

The gift of knowledge is given to increase our witness for Christ. It is not the same as extrasensory perception, called ESP. The Spirit gives His gifts through our spirit for our witness to Jesus. A great deal of knowledge about people obtained through the powers of the mind, such as ESP, can be a burden to the one receiving it, and it is knowledge that can be used very unwisely. The Spirit of God gives us only what we need to know. Although it is a correct knowledge, our understanding may be imperfect; but if it is from God, it will always be in agreement with the principles of the Word of God and will be attended with His peace in our hearts. We need to listen carefully and check to see whether what we have heard is from God. If a word of knowledge is given to a group, then it is the responsibility of the group to judge if it is from God.

This gift of knowledge may come in such a casual way that we hardly recognize it as of the Spirit. Sometimes when we pray for those in need, people will say, "How did you know to pray for that?" and we will have no idea how we knew. At other times, the Spirit may impress us in ways that many, including ourselves, will recognize. In all cases, let us be careful to follow the Spirit's leading. The Church has too long been embarrassed into silence, as it denied the supernatural power of God to speak today as He did in the New Testament days. For the tremendous task of bearing witness of Jesus Christ to every creature in every generation, we need the supernatural help of God, and Jesus promised the power of the Holy Spirit for that task.

Whereas the gift of wisdom may stand alone, and the gift of knowledge may be related to one gift or another, the gift of faith seems to be related to all the gifts of the Spirit. Faith does not stand alone, but demands that action springs from it; as James says, "...faith; if it does not lead to action, is in itself a lifeless thing" (NEB). Therefore, we will now consider faith briefly, and later relate it to the other gifts of the Spirit.

Faith is the channel through which God has chosen to work. God has never promised to answer prayer as such; He has only promised to answer believing prayer. Many prayers not only do no good, but also do much harm, as is illustrated by this incident. A mother put her two little girls to bed. She prayed with them, kissed them good night, and turned out the light. In the dark the little sister said, "I'm scared!"

"I'll pray for you," the older sister replied. So she prayed, "O Lord, don't let those wicked men that steal little children at night come and break into this house and take little sister away. And don't let the fierce animals come out of the woods and crawl into the window and frighten little sister." You know what was happening to the little sister? She was becoming more frightened with each prayer. So when we pray, telling God all about the big problems, we hinder both our faith and the one for whom we are praying. Faith sees what God sees and takes hold of that. It takes hold of the hand of God and the hand of the needy one, and so, provides the channel for the power of God to flow freely from God to man.

But we may ask, "How do we obtain faith?" Faith is a mysterious thing to the natural mind. It is not found by looking within oneself, for the closer we look, the less we find. Nor does faith spring up by self-scrutiny. Near my boyhood home is a deep canyon with a swinging bridge supported by cables stretched across it. As boys, we used to enjoy running over it, looking down several hundred feet to the walls of rock and the rushing stream below. We would try to get our elders to cross it, but they would hesitate. Would it have done any good to tell them to look inside themselves to see if they had faith enough to cross the bridge? No, that might only have increased their fears. But once they got their eyes on the bridge, the strength of the cables, how well they were anchored, and how easily the bridge carried others across, then they would begin to believe that it could carry them too.

So it is that faith grows in people, too. As we get acquainted with people and find them trustworthy, our faith in them begins to grow. At first, we might only trust them with one dollar, and that rather reluctantly. But as they prove their faithfulness, we would be willing to trust them with all that we have. Similarly, our faith in God grows as we become acquainted with Him. We get to know Him through the reading of the Scriptures, and "so faith comes from what is preached, and what is preached comes from the word of Christ" (Rom. 10:17). We get further acquainted with Him through the experience of others; but, most of all, we know God through our experience with Him.

God expects us to start where we are and trust Him for the little things, and when we find Him to be faithful, we will become bold enough to trust Him for something greater. God leads us gently, step by step, as a mother will teach her child to walk before she learns to run. Here may lie the difference between faith and presumption. David's words to Goliath might seem boastful:

Today Yahweh [Jehovah] *will deliver you into my hand and I shall kill you; I will cut off your head, and this very day I will give your dead body and the bodies of the Philistine army to the birds of the air and the wild beasts of the earth, so that all the earth may know that there is a God in Israel* (1 Samuel 17:46).

Yet, the words were not boastful, brash, or presumptuous because David already had found God to be faithful in his encounter with the lion and the bear. Now, he could trust God concerning Goliath. Faith is daring to step out where we can see no footing. Then God usually leads us to take only one step further than we have taken before.

The gift of faith by the Holy Spirit, then, is based upon our past experience with God, and is calling for obedience in the next step. Even though we may not feel that we are ready to take that step, God will give us faith for that for which He has prepared us.

I remember my feelings as I received a call, from the hospital, from a young couple whose child was critically ill. Of course, I would go to see these anxious parents. But before I could leave the telephone, I heard the Lord clearly saying, "Lay your hand on that child and I will heal him." I did not want to get into the "healing business," nor did I think I was prepared. In fact, I was quite afraid of getting involved in these things. However, God had done a work in my heart so that I knew that healing through prayer was valid, and when God gave me that clear impression to lay my hands upon that child for healing, He gave me faith with it. It was my obedience that was tested, not my faith, for He had given me faith for the occasion. Was I willing to risk my reputation and get involved? When I decided that I must go on in obedience, the faith was there and God did the healing.

What an encouragement it is that when God gives us the seemingly impossible assignment to preach the gospel to the whole world in each generation, He also gives supernatural power to do it. Jesus promised, "But you will receive power when the Holy Spirit comes on you, and then you will be my witnesses not only in Jerusalem but throughout Judaea and Samaria, and indeed to the ends of the earth" (Acts 1:8). We have foolishly tried to take up the assignment without the power.

The promise of Jesus implies that He will give us power to be effective witnesses to Him. When we are tried for our faith, we can expect God to give us supernatural wisdom that will overcome all the wisdom of man. When we are at a loss to know how to approach a problem, God may give us a word of knowledge that will strike right to the heart of the person in need and make the witness surprisingly effective. And when God gives us an assignment that is seemingly far too big for us, we may suddenly find that the faith for it is there and only obedience is needed. Then, we can know that God does not demand something from us that He has not already made provision for by His Holy Spirit.

Questions for Discussion

1. Where do you find the gifts of wisdom, knowledge, and faith illustrated in the life of Jesus and in the Book of Acts?

2. Where have you seen these gifts manifested in the Church today? How does faith come?

3. What do you think hinders Christians from exercising these gifts?

Chapter 6

The Gifts of Healing and Miracles

It was the need for healing of the little boy, Kenny, mentioned on the first page, that first made me consider the gifts of the Holy Spirit. In the ministry of healing, we get very near to people in their need. Perhaps this is the reason that Jesus did so much healing. He always met people at the point of their need and let the power of God touch them there; then, they would be encouraged to trust Him for further needs. We need to follow the example of Jesus and learn to do the works that He did. If we are willing to pray in faith for the sick, we will find that our opportunities for witness to Jesus Christ will increase greatly. One of the most common topics of people's casual conversation is their health, and we may begin right at this point of need to bring them to Jesus. We must again take the responsibility of healing that Jesus gave to the Church.

Knowing that Kenny had only a short time to live, his parents had turned to me. Since I was their pastor, this situation was something I could not avoid, and it proved to be a great learning experience. I began to find the difference between the prayer that ends with, "If it be Thy will," and the prayer that is based on finding the will of God first, and then praying according to it. I had stood by the bedside of the sick many times and prayed earnestly, "If it is your will then make this friend well." If he recovered, then I concluded it must have been God's will, and God had heard my prayer. If he did not, then it must have been God's will for him to die, and so I was absolved.

It is true that Jesus prayed, "If it is your will, take this cup away from me. Nevertheless let your will be done" (see Mt. 26:39). However, He already knew what the Father's will was, for He had told the disciples about it. But if we are not willing to find out what God's will is before we pray, we will not have much faith to believe.

I well remember the day when Alice, Kenny's mother, told me that Kenny had said to her, in the midst of one of his severe headaches, "Mommie, put your hand on my head and pray for me as Jesus did." It was a most natural thing for his mother to do, but it spelled something very different for me.

If I were to lay my hands on Kenny and pray for him, I knew that I would become very involved in the healing process. Perhaps God could use me if I believed Him, but it could be that I would be the resistant force hindering God's healing if I did not believe. That caused a great struggle in my soul. Did I want to get that closely involved in healing? If I wanted to be a help, then I needed to know that God wanted to heal, and that He wanted to use me. I began to realize that the question was not, "Can God heal?" Of course He can heal if He is God! But the real question was, "Can God heal through me?" That was very

108

personal and demanded a deep searching of my heart. It raised more questions.

The first question was, "Does God always want to heal?" For the answer to that question, I was forced to acknowledge a dichotomy in my thinking. When I wanted to pray for someone that was ill, I was unsure whether God really wanted to heal that person, so I added the phrase, "If it be Thy will." Now, if my child was ill, I had no hesitation about calling the doctor or having her take medicine; in fact, I knew I would seriously neglect my responsibility if I didn't do that. Innately, I knew it was God's will that she be well. So it was right to be healed through medicine, but somehow I felt that it might not be right to seek healing through prayer. I was making the doctor and medicine be the only determination of God's will, as though God wanted to heal only through medicine; and if medicine did not do its work, then it might be that God wanted my child to be sick. I saw how very wrong that was, for if God wanted to heal, then it was surely right to seek healing through prayer as well as through medical help.

At the same time, I was getting encouragement about the value of prayer for healing from the doctors them selves. Dr. Albert Heustis, the Health Commissioner for the State of Michigan, spoke to a group of pastors about the neglect of the Church in not taking its part in the healing ministry. He said that there were areas of healing that cannot be reached by medicine, but can only be reached by prayer. When I saw this noted medical doctor, who had been appointed by President John F. Kennedy to important national positions, on the same platform with Agnes Sanford, the wife of the late Edgar Sanford, an Episcopalian rector, who shared her experience of healing by prayer in a very practical, matter-of-fact way, I had to take a second look.

Perhaps, we were neglecting an important ministry that Jesus has called us to. Formerly, relying on the training I had received, I had said, "If one believed in healing, then no one should die." But it was the doctors that answered that question for me while I was taking a training course as a hospital chaplain. They said that disease should really not have anything to do with death, i.e., the proper way to die is in good health. This made me ask if we were not in the same position as Israel, when they were in the wilderness. God had said that if they would obey Him, then none of the diseases of the other nations would come upon them (see Ex. 15:26). God did not say they would not die. Death was not to be a consequence of disease, but a terminal point after a long life. So it was not according to God's plan that man be cut down by disease. Medicine was doing everything possible to eliminate the destructive effect of disease. Prayer, too, must play an important part in the process, or restoration, and maintenance of health. How important that part was, I was soon to find out.

One day, while I was temporarily serving as a chaplain at the Mt. Clemens General Hospital in a suburb of Detroit, the medical director greeted me with the words, "Oh Chaplain, I'm so glad that you have come. We need you." He explained that over 50 percent of the patients in this hospital had no organic problems, although they had pain (and the pain was real). By this, he inferred that over half of the patients admitted to the hospital should really be my responsibility as a chaplain, and not the doctors.

This was confirmed to me during a visit in Bangkok, Thailand, where a doctor spoke to me after my lecture on this subject. He said that in his first class as a medical student, the professor, a Harvard graduate, stated that 65 percent of the patients treated by medical doctors have no organic problems. The professor advised his students not to become medical doctors if they did not have their own emotional and spiritual problems solved. I concluded that doctors today are forced to carry much of the load that the Church has failed to carry!

One doctor said to me, "If I were to act in my practice like the Church does with healing, I would have given up long ago. If I give medicine to a patient and he doesn't get well, I don't decide that medicine doesn't work. I try another medicine. Many Christians try prayer, and if it doesn't work, they give up, instead of checking to see what was wrong and trying again."

Thus, while learning through the Holy Spirit and the doctors, we continued to pray for Kenny, and to listen. The doctors told us they could not heal the body only and leave the soul to the minister because man cannot be divided. The whole person must be dealt with.

In the Church we have tried to heal the soul without ministering to the body, and we have found that this is impossible. Jesus always dealt with the whole person, and so must we. Though sometimes the problems are too great for us to handle, we must do what we can.

Kenny had a rapidly developing tumorous cancer of the brain, and the doctors' prognosis was that he would have only two or three months to live. But, through the help of many, and principally through prayer, Kenny lived for four years. A great healing in his whole person took place during that time. He matured rapidly in his emotional and spiritual life so that he had many adult friends. He had such assurance in his trust in God, that he comforted his parents. On one occasion, he told them that Jesus could heal him, and if He didn't, then he was ready to die.

When death approached, the doctors tried to prepare the parents by warning them of the intense suffering Kenny would experience before his passing. However, the usually anticipated pattern which accompanied his type of condition nearing the end never manifested itself. I was at his bedside many times during his last days. He became weaker, and weaker, and gradually slipped away quietly and peacefully into the presence of the Lord.

Though the healing process that we were learning about was not able to surmount the great physical sickness that had taken hold, it did bring about, in the midst of his suffering, a great wholeness in Kenny's person. A wonderful healing and growth was taking place in his soul and spirit while the struggle in his physical body was being waged. I wish that Kenny would still be with us, but even in that loss I learned a lesson.

Later, in speaking of this experience to our board of deacons, one of whom was Kenny's father, I said, "We have some successes and some failures as we learn. I wish we had not failed with Kenny."

The father spoke up immediately, "Pastor, don't you ever call that a failure. God did some wonderful things through that experience." Thus, I was encouraged by the very one suffering the loss. It has taken away my fear to obey the Lord in prayer for the sick. When praying for health, we pray for the whole person—his or her physical, mental, and spiritual health. Whether a physical healing results or not, God always blesses. His blessing is not to the one prayed for alone, but to all who take part in faith. It was this experience that opened the door to me to learn about the power of God in ways that my doctrinal teaching had eliminated. It led me to experiences that I could hardly have imagined.

Jesus, by His example, taught us the importance of healing. Matthew tells us that Jesus "cured all who were sick" (Mt. 8:16), and went "curing all kinds of diseases and sickness" (Mt. 9:35). In the context of the first statement, it is implied that He healed all that came to Him. In the latter, we learn that there was no kind of disease that did not yield to His healing power.

He immediately taught His disciples to do the same. "He summoned his 12 disciples, and gave them authority...to cure all kinds of diseases and sickness" (Mt. 10:1). Then He said, "And as you go, proclaim that the kingdom of heaven is close at hand. Cure the sick, raise the dead, cleanse the lepers, cast out devils" (Mt. 10:7-8a). It was not the 12 only, but to the 70 He also said, "Cure those in it who are sick, and say, 'The kingdom of God is very near to you' " (Lk. 10:9). What the disciples were taught the Church practiced freely.

> *So many signs and wonders were worked among the people at the hands of the apostles...that the sick were even taken out into the streets and laid on beds and sleeping mats in the hope that at least the shadow of Peter might fall across some of them as he went past. People even came crowding in from the towns around about Jerusalem, bringing with them their sick and those tormented by unclean spirits, and all of them were cured* (Acts 5:12-16).

A similar kind of experience is recorded later concerning the apostle Paul's ministry (see Acts 19:11-12).

It is evident that healing was part of the ministry of Jesus and the early Church. However, we need to observe carefully how Jesus healed. In the Gospel records, we find important basic principles of healing upon which we should found our healing ministry. The physician Luke tells us that He "laid His hands on everyone of them, and healed them" (Lk. 4:40, KJV). The physical contact was important to many for "...everyone in the crowd was trying to touch him because power came out of him that cured them all" (Lk. 6:19). We remember the woman that touched the hem of His garment and was healed. For doing that, she was not rebuked but, rather, encouraged by Jesus.

There was a power that flowed through Jesus of which He was aware, and the sick people must have recognized it, for they were trying to touch Him. Many scientists are now beginning to realize that there is a healing power in the universe. A pastor's wife told of a committee of medical doctors, psychiatrists, and scientists at a leading hospital that asked her what she felt when she prayed for the sick. She said that sometimes she felt something and sometimes not, but the feeling had nothing to do with the healing. She called it vibration. The scientist said, "Do not call it vibration; call it radiation, for we know that there is a healing power in the universe, but we do not know how to contact or control it." It may be because Jesus knew that this power was flowing through Him that He laid His hands on them.

Later on, after Jesus had ascended into Heaven and the apostles were carrying on His work, the people saw such wonders happen through Peter that they tried to get as close as possible to him. But, apparently, the crowds were too great to allow that. They did the next best thing, in their minds, by taking the sick out on the streets in beds and mats so that Peter's shadow might touch them. We might have been prone to criticize them for their superstition, but God healed them. It seems that during the apostle Paul's ministry, the people could not even bring the sick near him so "that handkerchiefs or aprons which had touched him were taken to the sick, and they were cured of their illnesses… " (Acts 19:12). Evidently, God uses any means that will encourage a true outreach of faith to His power. Jesus probably used clay on the eyes of the blind man, and the washing in the pool, to strengthen the man's faith (see Jn. 9:6-7).

Here is an example from the present day. In a church where healing by faith was not practiced, the following incident took place that shook the traditional foundations of some in the city I was visiting. A woman, with a serious problem in her leg was listening to a radio pastor. She heard him say, "Put your hand on the radio while I pray." She did that, evidently reaching out in faith as she did so. Instantly, her leg was healed. This so affected her cursing, swearing husband that he was saved, and the testimony of them both moved the church. It was God who healed her and saved her husband, but it was her simple, and seemingly foolish, act of reaching out that provided the means by which her faith could take hold of the promise of God.

Mark tells us that when Jesus sent out the 12 in pairs, they "anointed many sick people with oil and cured them" (Mk. 6:13b). Later James says, "If one of you is ill, he should send for the elders of the church, and they must anoint him with oil in the name of the Lord and pray over him. The prayer of faith will save the sick man and the Lord will raise him up again…" (Jas. 5:14-15).

Here we need, also, to recognize the doctors, the instruments of all the healing arts, as the means upon which we have so depended for the maintenance of health. They are gifts from God; for they have studied the body and the causes of illness, and thereby, they have been a means of saving countless lives. We would do them a favor by practicing more preventative health care.

God honors the means as long as it remains an outreach of our faith, and does not become an object that we venerate. We see this illustrated in one of the Old Testament stories (see Num. 21). When God sent the poisonous serpents to bite the people because of their complaining, they repented and confessed their sin. Then God told Moses to make a bronze replica of one of those serpents so that whoever was bitten and looked upon it would be healed. We know that the bronze serpent had no healing power, but it was God's means to encourage faith. However, when that same bronze serpent became an object of veneration, it was destroyed (see 2 Kings 18:4). Hezekiah, we are told, broke it up because the people had begun to burn incense before it and worship it. Faith is to be attached only to the living God, though it may be encouraged by tangible means.

Physical contact, however, is not always needed for healing. Jesus did not lay His hands upon all. We are told of His remarkable experience with the Roman centurion. Jesus offered to go and cure his servant, probably by laying hands on him; but the officer said, "Sir, I am not worthy to have you under my roof; just give the word and my servant will be cured." Surely this great humility and faith pleased Jesus more than the eagerness of the crowd, for He said, "Nowhere in Israel have I found faith like this" (see Mt. 8:8,10). Hereby, He indicates that if faith is great enough, the human touch may not be needed; such a personal contact may only be an encouragement to faith.

Faith is most prominent in Jesus' healing ministry. He acted on faith in God and called forth the faith of those who wanted help. Faith is the channel through which the power of God flows. The father who cried out in desperation for his boy said, "If it is at all possible—help us."

"If it is at all possible," said Jesus. "Everything is possible to the one who has faith." (See Mark 9:20-25.) Jesus called forth as much faith as possible from the one seeking help, yet the greater faith was His. So it should be with us as we seek to help others. We simply join our faith to the faith, be it ever so small, of the one who is asking for help, and we offer that as a channel for God's power. As Jesus said, "...if two of you on earth agree to ask anything at all, it will be granted to you by my Father in heaven. For where two or three meet in my name, I shall be there with them" (Mt. 18:19-20). Jesus said that though our faith is like a grain of mustard seed, we can command the mountain to move.

Faith is seeing the invisible, so that the one who prays in faith sees what God sees and acts on it. He sees not primarily the sickness or disease but the health that God sees for the sick one. There is an expression of Jesus in the performance of two of His miracles that seems to imply this kind of trust and confidence in His heavenly Father. When He was implored by the president of the synagogue, "My daughter has just died, but come and lay your hand on her, and her life will be saved," Jesus, evidently, held onto her life in faith, even saying to the mourners, "The little girl is not dead, she is asleep," and was scornfully laughed at for it. Although He knew she was dead, He held on to her life in faith, not even admitting death to those who had come to mourn. Because His faith did not fail, she was raised from the dead. (See Matthew 9:18-26.) Jesus did this again with Lazarus. He told the disciples that Lazarus had fallen asleep and that He would awaken him, but then had to explain to them that Lazarus was already dead. Again Jesus seemed to be holding on to that which He saw by faith, while everyone around Him saw only death and defeat. He still held on when He learned that Lazarus had been dead four days already, and His friends were blaming Him. What persistence in faith! It was not a selfish persistence, but a persistence against all unbelief. This kind of trust looks foolish in the eyes of others because they do not see what faith sees.

With this kind of faith, we can give thanks before receiving the answer. Jesus said, "I tell you therefore: everything you ask for, believe that you have it already, and it will be yours" (Mk. 11:24). When we are led by the Spirit of God to ask for that which God tells us is in accordance with His will, then we need ask only once and accept it in faith, giving thanks that it is done. When I was called to the hospital to see the child that I told of in Chapter 5, I knew that God had promised healing and that He would do it. Therefore, I could only ask once and continue to give thanks afterward, even though I received word that the child was much worse. As we gave thanks together, the healing process, which the doctor could not account for, began. Notice that Jesus says, "Believe that you have it already and it will be yours." This indicates that we are to give thanks when we believe, before we see the healing.

I will give an illustration that is extreme, but for that reason it will illustrate this point well. A woman in our city had a goiter that was large and could be plainly seen. She asked for prayer for healing and believed that she had received the answer, so she began to give thanks, even though there was no physical change. However, her friends could only see the goiter and not her faith, so they began to look upon her as acting very foolishly. One day, she said to the Lord, "I know that you have healed me." (That is, the promise was taken as though it was completed.) "But this bothers people, so for their sakes, please take care of it." Suddenly, as she was walking across the street, she noticed that her goiter was gone. (If this sounds extreme, remember that Alexis Carrol, the great scientist, says that he saw a tumor dissolve under his eyes, through prayer.) If God can be trusted to fulfill His promises, then we can begin to give Him thanks as soon as He has given us His word.

The Lord laid down guidelines to all healing for the Israelites:

If you listen carefully to the voice of Yahweh your God and do what is right in his eyes, if you pay attention to his commandments and keep his statutes, I shall inflict on you none of the evil [diseases] *that I inflicted on the Egyptians, for it is I, Yahweh who give you healing* (Exodus 15:26).

It is important that our prayer for the health of a person relate to all the areas—physical, mental, emotional, and spiritual—in that person's life, so that we can bring all of his faculties into harmony with the laws of God in His creation. We need, also, to listen for whatever truth there is in any of the healing arts. To avoid certain areas of knowledge is to prevent God's power from operating in a manner that He may choose. Healing by prayer is a means by which God can operate in people, as is healing by medicine, or osteopathy, or chiropractic, or any other of the healing arts; all healing comes only from God as He is the source of life. Openness to every truth in the area of healing is as necessary as openness to whatever truth there may be in the doctrines of various denominations. It is important that no prejudice be allowed to stand in the way of God's truth in any realm.

Once again, "I will put none of these diseases upon thee...for I am the Lord that healeth thee." Jesus fulfills and amplifies His Father's commands in both word and work, and by His example He directs us to do likewise. On the whole, we are just beginning to understand again this command of our God. We are just beginning, too, to understand the effects that the full living out of these commands can have in the realm of the healing of psychosomatic illnesses; and in the same vein, how such illnesses can be healed through the prayer of faith.

Through prayer, God may reach deeply buried memories in a person's life and, thus, heal the infection of deep resentments. Through medicine, the infection of a wound may be stopped so that healing may take place. Through chiropractic aid, the impairment of the nerves of the spine may be relieved and allow the healing life to flow through the whole body. Though we are, admittedly, at the beginnings of such understanding; nevertheless, we can set no limit upon God's healing power because we do not understand His ways. But because our understanding is limited, we must not cease trying to recognize the truth inherent in healing, through both prayer and all the healing arts.

We have noted that Jesus healed all that came to Him, and He healed all kinds of sicknesses and diseases, yet He did not heal everyone. You will remember that there were "crowds of sick people—blind, lame, paralyzed" at the pool of Bethesda (see Jn. 5:4), but Jesus healed only one man. He healed only those who wanted to be healed by Him, and, in this instance, this man was evidently the only one who looked to Him for help. We are not called upon to empty the hospitals. I found less opportunity to pray for the physical healing of the sick in the hospital while I was a chaplain than when I worked outside. The reason is that the hospital was built for medical care, and the patients looked to the doctor and medicine for healing. Therefore, it was not my place to interfere with what was being done, but I gave my attention to the emotional and spiritual needs of the patients. Jesus asked blind Bartimaeus, who was calling to Him to have mercy upon him, "What do you want me to do for you?" (Mk. 10:51) Bartimaeus needed to be specific concerning his need and request. It seems to be quite evident that Jesus healed only those who came to Him and wanted His help, and this is good counsel for us.

However, at times we need even more specific guidance. Jesus said of himself, "he can do only what he sees the Father doing: and whatever the Father does, the Son does too" (Jn. 5:19b). The key to faith is to know what God wants us to do. The great men of prayer, such as George Müller and Andrew Murray, said that they spent much more time in finding guidance concerning the will of God than in praying for the need. If we do not know what God wants to do, then it is hard to believe that God will answer our prayer. Furthermore, we must determine just what God's will is concerning the need. Does He want to meet the spiritual or the physical need first? Is there need of removal of emotional barriers to healing? Does God want us or someone else to meet this need?

In Papua New Guinea, as the translators working with the primitive tribes began to pray for the sick to be healed, they were greatly encouraged. In a tribal village, an anxious mother came to the translator with her little child who had spinal meningitis. The infant's neck was already stiff and his head thrown back. The translator was eager to pray for the child, but she wisely asked guidance from God. The answer that she received was "No," and she was puzzled and asked again. However, she received no liberty to pray. So she sent for the Christian man of the village, asking him to take the mother and child to the hospital. However, this man, not knowing what had transpired and having seen the power of God at work in healing before, laid his hands upon the child and prayed. Immediately, the child relaxed, his head came forward, and he began to nurse at his mother's breast. God, evidently, wanted this tribal man to be used by Him for the healing of the child.

Perhaps the greatest miracle of healing in which I have participated came when my faith was smallest. Once, when we had just returned to South America, a couple asked if we would pray for their daughter, Betsy, for she was very ill. Her case was clinically diagnosed as periarteritis, which is often fatal shortly after diagnosis. She had been ill for some time. As I came into her room, I asked, "Betsy, do you believe that God would heal you now if I would pray for you?" She said that she wished that she could, but that she was unable to, for she had been, and was still, so sick and people had already prayed very much for her. I said that I could not pray for her instantaneous healing either, for my faith was not big enough, and no good wishes, or sympathy or presumption could replace faith. So I asked what was one of her needs, that we could pray for it and believe God together. She said that she could not sleep well, and so I asked whether she thought God wanted to give her a good night's rest. She said, "Yes," and we agreed that we could believe God for that.

Our faith was not big enough to ask for complete healing, but it was enough for the good night's sleep, and God accepted our small faith. When the night came, she felt very hot (sometimes evident in healing), but when her mother took her temperature, it was normal. In the morning, she felt good and her faith increased; and I went away encouraged, for healing had begun, though it seemed to be a slow process. Actually, she was sick for several years after the prayer, and the symptoms persisted. However, later the doctors discovered that the cortisone that she continued to take after our prayer was causing her continued illness. When they took her off the medication, she soon became well. It was then that they discovered that she had been completely healed of her serious illness at the time of the prayer. At that time, however, we should have asked for God's guidance concerning the next step after prayer. We should not ignore the doctor, but perhaps, we should make him aware that we have introduced another factor in the healing process.

If it is important to see the Holy Spirit's guidance concerning specific instruction before we pray, then we need to answer the common question, "How do you recognize God's voice among all the voices that cry with us; for example, our desires, public opinion, satan's subtle deceitfulness, etc.?" It is not the place for us to speak fully about this subject, but it seems necessary to make a few suggstions. I can no more tell you how to recognize God's voice than I can tell you how to recognize your mother's voice. Your mother's voice is as specific as your fingerprint; her voice was printed on your memory when you first heard it. God's voice was printed on your spirit when you became a child of God by faith in Christ. Jesus said, "The sheep that belong to me listen to my voice... " (Jn. 10:27). However, the rationalistic teaching that says we cannot really know the will of God may have dimmed its clarity. Then it becomes necessary to come to God as a little child and ask Him to protect us from unnecessary mistakes and overrule the necessary ones as we venture in obedience to that which we think is the voice of God. We will make mistakes, but God will correct us with the kind of love and care that a mother has as she watches her child take his first step. Of course, he will fall, but he will learn only by trying; so we learn to recognize the voice of God again by obeying.

As we learn to recognize the voice of God and under stand His will more specifically, our prayer changes. We no longer pray for the sick, saying, "If it be Thy will," for these words indicate that we have not determined His will. With that deadening phrase, we seek to absolve ourselves from all responsibility and put it upon God. If the sick get well, we say it was God's will; and if they die, it was God's will. Yet Jesus says, "If you have faith," then His work shall be done. God is calling upon us to take up the responsibility of learning to know His will, and of then believing Him so that it shall be done. We would not keep an employee long who never really bothers to find out what he is supposed to do. It is a sign of immaturity in our Christian life if we do not know the specific direction of our ministry. The whole of Scripture is a record of men and women who learned to know what the will of God was for them and did it.

If we are to do the works that Jesus did, then we must also heal the sick. Jesus always treated sickness as an enemy, as also the doctors do. He never consoled anyone by saying that his or her sickness was given by God, and that that individual should be happy in it. Sickness came into the world with sin, and has been closely associated with it ever since. In the midst of the record of Jesus' great healing ministry, the writer Matthew included the healing of sickness in Jesus' great work of redemption on the cross: "He cast out the spirits with a word and cured all who were sick, to fulfill the prophecy of Isaiah: 'He took our sicknesses away and carried our diseases for us' [Is. 53:4]" (Mt. 8:16b-17). Furthermore, the very word "save" in Scripture is the same word that means to heal or to make whole.

We innately know that it is God's will for us to be well, for in a critical illness we do not hesitate to call the doctor or take medicine. It is only when we pray that we question whether it is God's will. The general rule in the New Testament is that all who wanted healing were healed; the exceptions to that rule are only one or two, such as Epaphras who was left sick in Miletus, for reasons that we do not know; and Paul's "thorn in the flesh," which may or may not have been physical, though we know it was given to him by God to keep him from pride.

As we seek to heal the sick, we will have many more exceptions than that, but let us not make exceptions of Scripture the rule of our lives. Let us be open to the gift of healing so that those who want to be healed may see the power of God.

Some say that if healing were for today, then no one would die. It was rather surprising to me, as I have mentioned before, to hear doctors say to hospital chaplains that the proper way to die is while still in good health, not through disease. So, death will come in its time even in good health. When God told Moses that if Israel would obey God's laws then none of the sicknesses that plagued Egypt would come upon them, He did not say that they would not die. We stand in a similar position today.

The greatest barrier to healing is unbelief. A medical doctor in Pakistan said that she knew without question that God healed through prayer, for she had seen it in the healing meetings held there. But the question that bothered her was why the lame and blind should come to those meetings with great expectation and go home disappointed. The answer to that difficult question seems to be given to us from Jesus' own ministry.

Mark tells us that in his hometown, Jesus "...could work no miracle there, though he cured a few sick people by laying hands on them. He was amazed at their lack of faith" (Mk. 6:5-6). If Jesus could not perform any great miracles because of the unbelief of the people around Him, then we should not be surprised that we cannot do any more. Unbelief is not only an absence of faith, but it is also a definite barrier to the power of God. When Jesus went to raise Jairus' daughter from the dead, He first put out the unbelievers and took in with Him those disciples who could help provide the channel of faith. This is a good example to follow if we want to see God at work in healing.

May we so provide channels of faith that we produce an atmosphere of faith for God to do His work.

Madame Guyon, a member of the nobility of France in its earlier history, and a great woman of prayer, tells of her experience with the healing of a sick girl.

"This girl fell grievously sick. I was willing to give her assistance in my power, but I found I had nothing to do but to command her bodily sickness, or the disposition of her mind; all that I said was done. It was then that I learned what it was to command by the Word, and to obey by the Word. It was Jesus Christ in me, equally commanding and obeying.

"She, however, continued sick for some time. One day, after dinner, I was moved to say to her, 'Rise and be no longer sick.' She arose and was cured. The nuns were very much astonished. They knew nothing of what had passed, but saw her walking, who in the morning had appeared to be in the last extremity. They attributed her disorder to a vivid imagination.

"I have at sundry times experienced, and felt in myself. how much God respects the freedom of man, even demands his free concurrence; for when I said, 'Be healed,' or 'Be free from your troubles,' if such persons acquiesced the Word was efficacious, and they were healed. If they doubted, or resisted, though under fair pretexts, saying, 'I shall be healed when it pleases God; I will not be healed till He wills it'; or in the way of despair, 'I cannot be healed; I will not quit my condition,' then the Word had no effect. I felt in myself that the divine virtue returned in me. I experienced what our Lord said when the woman afflicted with the issue of blood touched

Him. He instantly asked, 'Who touched me?' The apostles said, 'Master, the multitude throng thee, and press thee; and sayest thou, "Who touched me?" ' He replied, 'It is because virtue hath gone out of me' (Lk. 8:45-46). Jesus Christ had caused that healing virtue to flow, through me, by means of His Word. When that virtue met not with a correspondence in the subject, I felt it suspended in its source. That gave me some pain. I should be, as it were, displeased with those persons; but when there was no resistance, but a full acquiescence, this divine virtue had its full effect. Healing virtue has so much power over things inanimate, yet the least thing in man either restrains it, or stops it entirely."[1]

In all of our experience, we must be humble and willing to learn, for most of us are just beginners. We must acknowledge our limitations, be honest about our mistakes, and be willing to learn. We may pray in the case of our own illness, and if we are not healed, we may ask another to pray for us, or several who are agreed in prayer. If that channel is not sufficient, we may call for the elders of the church, be anointed with oil, and believe God until we see His power or hear His word of instruction.

There are many laws or principles of prayer that are interrelated and need to be taken into consideration. The mother of some of our Christian friends was a very fine person, but had no joy or assurance of salvation. One day, the doctors found that she had inoperable cancer. The news was a great shock, but she decided to seek God's help. Her son-in-law told her that if she wanted prayer,

---

1. Madame Guyon, *Madame Guyon (autobiography)*, (Chicago: Moody Press, 1920), 283-284.

she would have to forgive her husband. Not knowing of this, I felt impelled to say the same thing to her. (Her husband had left her, after she had borne 12 children, and had married twice since, coming into some wealth.) She had much to forgive, but Jesus' law of prayer includes forgiving all others. It was a struggle, but she decided to forgive. Instantly, healing began in her soul, where the deepest healing begins. She had great assurance of her salvation and a joyous testimony for Christ. Then she asked for the elders of the church to anoint her with oil and pray for her. We invited those who could believe God for healing to join us, and God graciously gave us a gift of faith. After prayer, we suggested that she follow the doctor's directions. He prescribed cobalt treatments, and soon she was feeling so good that he spoke of her as the "miracle woman."

She went to share her radiant testimony with her 8 living children in several states, only two of whom were in the Church. After a year's time, she came home, having carried a great witness for Christ, fell ill, and was taken to the hospital. We did not feel that we should pray as we had before. Quietly, she slipped away without any of the distress that had been predicted. Was she healed? I would say, marvelously so! She was healed in her soul; then she was sufficiently healed in her body to share her witness with her family, and at 75 years of age, she went home to be with her Lord.

Many laws of prayer and healing were combined in that battle against our great enemies. So let us venture to obey God and allow Him to teach us to exercise the gift of healing as a witness to the saving power of God.

The gift of miracles may be differentiated from the gift of healing in that its specific reference seems to be to natural wonders, such as turning water into wine, stilling storms, walking on water, multiplying bread, etc. The concept of miracles that sees God overruling the laws of nature does not seem to be consistent with His design, for the laws of God operate through all reality—both material and spiritual. This may be illustrated by the material law of aerodynamics. One hundred years ago, the best scientist, if he had seen one of our great planes, would have said, "It cannot fly. The laws of gravity do not permit it." Have we done away with the laws of gravity? Not at all. We have discovered other laws concerning matter that allow us to overcome the law of gravity.

So, also, it is in the spiritual realm. Material laws are not abrogated by "miracles," but the laws of the spirit overcome them. The gift of miracles does not have to do with God's intervention in nature apart from us, but through us, in our discovery of spiritual laws by which we move upon material things. This is based on the place God gave to man in creation. God said,

> *"Let us make man in our image, in the likeness of ourselves, and let them be masters of the fish of the sea, the birds of heaven, the cattle, all the wild beasts and all the reptiles that crawl upon the earth." God created man in the image of himself, ... God blessed them, saying to them, "Be fruitful, multiply, fill the earth and conquer it. Be masters of the fish of the sea, the birds of heaven and all living animals on the earth"* (Genesis 1:26-28).

However, humankind lost that place of dominion through sin so that we have been out of harmony with nature ever since. But Jesus restored humanity to that place again. He spoke directly to the wind and the waves, and they obeyed Him. He was able to control the fish of the sea, and change the elements of water into wine. He told us to do the same when He said, "If your faith were the size of a mustard seed you could say to this mountain, 'Move from here to there,' and it would move; nothing would be impossible for you" (Mt. 17:20b). Again He said, "You could say to this mulberry tree, 'Be uprooted and planted in the sea,' and it would obey you" (Lk. 17:6). He did not say that we should ask God to perform miracles, but that we should speak to creation itself, and it would obey us as those that have ruled over it. St. Francis of Assisi demonstrated this great understanding and deep relationship with creation, as did Saddhu Sundar Singh, the Indian Christian holy man. Some have learned the language of the animal world to a remarkable degree, as is illustrated by J. Allen Boone in his books, *Kinship with Life* and *The Language of Silence*.

Science is beginning to show us our very close relationship with the plant world. We are finding out that it is not the "green thumb" that makes plants to grow but "the loving heart." I quote here Franklin Peterson's description of the work of Cleve Backster—for 22 years a lie detector technician, and called upon as an expert witness by congressional committees:

"For the past five years, polygraph expert Cleve Backster has been making lie detector studies of philodendrons in an effort to discover whether there is such a thing as an emotional experience for a plant. His data indicates that laboratory plants have displayed a surprising variety of reactions to the different types of stimulation he has subjected them to. Backster, who derives his livelihood from operating the Cleve Backster School of Lie Detection in New York, recently performed an experiment with six of his students in which they drew lots to see which one would kill a philodendron plant. The student with the secret assignment was to do the job without the knowledge of the others—entering the laboratory at night—pull the plant out of the pot by its roots and tear it apart, bit by bit. The next day, Backster attached the polygraph to the crime's only witness, an adjacent philodendron. The machine registered no emotional changes in the plant as five of the students entered the room, but in the presence of the murderer, the graph was a picture of intense agitation. The machine's finding was finally confirmed when the plant's killer admitted his guilt."[2]

If we have such a close relationship to the plant and animal world, then we had better learn to rule the world under God's guidance.

All of these laws and principles, especially those explicitly in the Scriptures, have opened up amazing new avenues of discovery for me. As I began to experience the power of God in healing through my hands, I felt as though I was living back in the New Testament days. The teachings and ministry of Jesus began to live before me. I found that I did not have to imagine myself living in that day, but that I need only allow the life of Jesus to be lived again in me. I suddenly discovered a new aspect of the theme of Paul's letters, "Christ in me." Oh, indeed, there was lots of resistance in me to hinder God's power, and I needed much refinement in guidance, but at least the power of God was really in evidence at times, so much so

---

2.   *Wall Street Journal*, February 2, 1972.

that it humbled me to think that God would actually show such power through such an insignificant vessel. And yet, there was so much more to discover.

Questions for Discussion

1. Why are people hesitant about praying for the sick, even though they are quite ready to call for the doctor or take medicine?

2. What is a prerequisite to praying for healing?

3. How did Jesus heal? What were some of His ways?

Chapter 7

The Gift of
Discernment of Spirits

While we were in Ecuador, missionary friends told us of a guest they had entertained in their upper Amazonian jungle home. The guest was one of the directors of a noted anthropological museum in the United States. He was doing some anthropological studies concerning a primitive tribe of Indians in Ecuador and Peru. In order to complete his studies, he felt that it was necessary for him to learn about the powers that the witch doctors claimed to have through their witchcraft. The anthropologist himself had disclaimed any faith in any supernatural forces. After his experiment, he returned home and a year later visited the missionary again, at which time he told his experience.

He had taken the Ayuasca drink that the Indians take in order to make contact with demon powers, and as he did so, he went into a very deep trance, during which he saw demons. The missionary said, "How did you know they were demons? You did not believe in demons."

"Oh, I know they were demons. There was no question about it. They were horrible, filthy things, and I saw their faces!" He said that he asked the demons, as witch doctors would, to do things for him; some of which they were able to do and some not. The drink that put him into a trance had left his mind somewhat hazy, even after a year's time. He then asked the missionary, "What is it that you do when you pray? Do you try to get in touch with God?"

"Yes," said the missionary friend, "that is what we do. "

In this day, many are seeking to make contact with the spiritual world through spiritualism, the Eastern religions, various forms of the occult, and drugs. They may, however, be shocked to find that there is more to the spiritual realm than they had anticipated. It is the realm of both God and satan, and related to it are powers than can either be directed by God for good, or by satan to bring a curse upon man. God knows that we cannot go safely through this realm alone, for we will be deceived and enslaved by the evil forces of satan, as the nations were in Moses' day. Therefore, God commanded Israel,

> *When you come into the land Yahweh your God gives you, you must not fall into the habit of imitating the detestable practices of the natives. There must never be anyone among you who makes his son or daughter pass through fire, who practices divination, who is soothsayer, augur or sorcerer, who uses charms, consults ghosts or spirits, or calls up the dead. For the man who does these things is detestable to Yahweh your God: it is because of these detestable practices that Yahweh your God is driving these nations before you* (Deuteronomy 18:9-12).

God provides us with an escort, Jesus, His Son, who conquered all satan's forces. He will lead us through the lower realms of psychic forces and demonic power to the holy place where God reigns alone. He wants us to have full fellowship with God and wants to empower us by His Holy Spirit so that we can deliver those who are enslaved by satan.

Many young people are opening their deep unconscious selves to satanic forces through drugs; others are playing with ouija boards and experimenting with seances, not knowing what forces they are dealing with. As we move into the spiritual realm, we proceed toward conflict. We need to know clearly who our friends and our enemies are. We cannot distinguish them with our physical senses, for their distinctions are spiritual, and the discernment between the good and evil is made through spiritual senses. Paul says, "For it is not against human enemies that we have to struggle, but against the Sovereignties and the Powers who originate the darkness in this world, the spiritual army of evil in the heavens" (Eph. 6:12), and "We live in the flesh, of course, but the muscles that we fight with are not flesh. Our war is not fought with weapons of flesh, yet they are strong enough, in God's cause, to demolish fortresses" (2 Cor. 10:3-4). It is for this reason that the Holy Spirit gives the gift of discernment of spirits.

Humankind becomes the battleground between God and satan. The serpent has managed to persuade people to sin; therefore, God wants to rescue them from sin's awful destruction. Sin is the violation of God's laws, upon which the whole of material and spiritual creation depends. The devil's snare would bring humankind to spiritual, physical, and finally, eternal death; God's desire for people is that they enjoy full physical, spiritual, and eternal life. We can, therefore, appreciate why we need to discern the spiritual powers that are operating all around.

Job's life is an example of the battle between God and satan. God challenged satan to consider His faithful servant, Job, who was blameless in his obedience to Him. Satan countered that it was because God had so blessed and protected Job that he could not be touched, and said that was why he trusted in God. God, therefore, allowed satan to take all that Job had, but not to touch him. Satan then took everything away from Job, even his children. But Job continued to trust in God. Again, satan reported to God and was challenged concerning Job's blameless life. This time satan said that Job's trust in God continued because he still had his health; whereupon, God gave satan permission to touch that also. When Job was then filled with running sores from head to foot, his faith was put to the highest test. God won in that battle because Job believed God, though he could see no reason for such great calamities befalling him. In this great drama, we see that satan is not omnipotent, omnipresent, or omniscient, for he has to report to God and can do only what God permits. This knowledge helps us in our dealing with the devil, who goes about like a roaring lion as though he was to be feared more than God.

Sin entered the human race, so the battle against sin must be fought in the human realm. That is why God became flesh in the person of His Son Jesus Christ. "Since all the children share the same blood and flesh, he too shared equally in it, so that by his death he could take away all the power of the devil, who had power over death, and set free all those who had been held in slavery all their lives by the fear of death" (Heb. 2:14-15). Jesus lived a completely human life: "For it is not as if we had a high priest who was incapable of feeling our weaknesses with us; but we have one who has been tempted in every way that we are, though he is without sin" (Heb. 4:15).

Because He had not sinned, Jesus could say that satan had no hold on Him. Thus, as a man, He took up the battle against sin and remained blameless, in spite of all the temptations satan put before Him. Therein, He completely defeated satan. "And so he got rid of the Sovereignties and the Powers, and paraded them in public, behind him in his triumphal procession" (Col. 2:15).

By His perfect life, Jesus Christ became the sacrifice for our sins, and unites us in victory through His resurrection over death. Therefore, in His name we can triumph over the devil. We have been adopted as sons in the family of God. Jesus allows us to use His name, which has authority and power in heaven and earth. We are raised to the right hand of God with Jesus and find a place in the heavenly realms. Even the angels are sent to assist us.

God, the God of hosts and armies of heaven, sends His angels to protect, guide, comfort, and help us. In a similar way, satan, the commander of multitudes of angels who revolted against God, seeks to deceive and destroy mankind by means of these fallen angels, evil spirits, demons. If we put ourselves under the care of God, we can expect the help of the angel spirits who serve God. On the other hand, if we rebel against God, we can expect to be deceived by satan and his evil spirits. This is well illustrated in *Screwtape Letters* by C.S. Lewis.

I am aware that some regard satan as a personification of a psychological power that is at work in each of us because we cannot escape from our own psyches; or a name for everything belonging to the self that we do not like as Christians. However, I prefer to remain with the simple scriptural description that presents satan and his spirits as personal, rather than psychological, forces. I believe this is an accurate description based on a more profound anthropology than ours, and it presents a practical approach to people's problems where they relate to spiritual powers. If possible, satan will attempt to conceal his identity, to hide under an assumed name. It is well known that in ancient religions when a subtle force had to name itself it lost its power, even as an unnamed fear may lose its power when we identify it. It is, perhaps, for this reason that Jesus called upon certain spirits to name themselves, and when they did so, they soon were cast out.

The description of the activity of evil spirits begins early in the biblical record. We are told that Cain was very angry with Abel because the latter's offering was received by God and his own was not. Then God warned him, "If you are well disposed, ought you not to lift up your head? But if you are ill disposed, is not sin at the door like a crouching beast hungering for you, which you must master?" (Gen. 4:7) Cain's anger was sin, and if sin was not mastered, then the "beast" or "demon," as it is called in another translation, would spring upon him and overpower him.

This is an accurate description of many a person's experience. He may commit a sin that he thinks he can easily overcome, but suddenly he finds that he is mastered by it and cannot free himself. This binding power is stronger than habit, for it is in a spiritual realm. A psychiatrist friend said that he knows, from his experience, that there are demons that cause people to do things that they ordinarily would not do at all. It was the "demon" that caused

Cain to kill his brother. We may find a crime of an otherwise good person inexplicable apart from outside forces working upon him. In other cases, people are bound to habits, caused to do foolish things, or held in fear or depression from which they cannot free themselves. However, we must be careful not to ascribe such symptoms as necessarily spirit-induced; rather, we should try to learn how to receive discernment concerning them.

Many people, out of curiosity or sorrow seek to communicate with the dead through witches or mediums and are deceived by evil spirits, as was King Saul (see 1 Sam. 28). Saul had received much counsel from God through Samuel, but now Samuel was dead, and Saul was in greater trouble than ever. It seems that he had never learned how to communicate with God, and now he was desperate for help. He, therefore, tried to get God's help through Samuel by communicating with the dead through a witch or medium. This was a practice strictly forbidden by God. When the medium sought to fulfill Saul's request, God intervened and brought up Samuel in an unusual way that horrified the medium; and, instead of comforting Saul, Samuel predicted his death. In fact, the scriptural record tells us,

> *Saul died because he had shown himself unfaithful to Yahweh: he had not kept the word of Yahweh; he had even questioned and consulted a necromancer. He had not consulted Yahweh, who therefore put him to death and transferred the monarchy to David son of Jesse"* (1 Chronicles 10:13-14).

A former medium who became a Christian described how people may be deceived in trying to communicate with the dead; rather than getting the help and comfort that the Holy Spirit can give. The deception, he said, comes through the "familiar spirit" of which the Bible speaks (the spirit under satan's control that is familiar with the former life of the deceased), through whom the medium or witch obtains her information. At first, as the man approaches the medium, he may doubt whether she (for most mediums are women) can really communicate with the dead. So the medium assures the man that she will prove, at their next appointment, that she has really been in communication with the deceased relative. To do this she goes into a trance in which she communicates with the "familiar spirit."

Through this spirit, she obtains intimate information concerning the deceased relative by which she persuades the man that she did indeed talk to the deceased one, though in reality she has not been in contact with that person at all, but only with the "familiar spirit." Armed with this intimate information about the deceased, she persuades the man that she can talk to his relative. The medium then goes into a trance and invites the man to talk to his relative through her. However, the answers that come through the medium, again, come from the "familiar spirit" under satan's control; and though they may be partly true, in the end they will deceive him. When ministering to African pastors in the interior of the country, I learned that witch doctors use exactly the same method to deceive their people.

There are many kinds of spirits named in the Bible record, and personal experience in this field quickly increases that number. It seems that the names given to spirits are according to the activities they carry on. Thus, we have the description of the lying spirits who persuaded Ahab to go into battle (see 1 Kings 22). A "behind the scenes" view is given to us of the spirits' activities in these Scriptures. The picture, symbolic or literal, shows us that these spirits reported to God and were given permission to make that wicked King Ahab fall. By being lying spirits in the mouths of all the prophets, they made them all speak unanimously of Ahab's coming success in battle, but the godly king, Jehoshaphat, still discerned that there was something wrong. Thus we can see that if public opinion is swayed by spirits of the enemy, the Christian can still recognize the voice of God from the crowd.

In the New Testament, we are told of a slave girl who had a spirit that enabled her to tell fortunes, and by this means make money for her masters. Paul rebuked that spirit and set the girl free to the chagrin of her masters who cared more for the money than the freedom of a slave girl (see Acts 16). Paul later warned Timothy of deceiving spirits who, evidently, would even try to work in the Church (see 1 Tim. 4:1). In the Gospel records and in the Book of Acts there are frequent references made to unclean spirits, which may indicate that this is a general term.

Then there are spirits that are associated with illnesses. When Jesus came to help the man whose boy seemed to have the symptoms that we associate with an epileptic, He recognized the spirits of uncleanness, deafness and muteness, and cast them out so that the boy was well (see Mk. 9:14-29). Luke, the physician, tells of a woman "possessed by a spirit that left her enfeebled; she was bent double and quite unable to stand upright." Jesus, after setting her free, speaks of her as "a daughter of Abraham whom satan has held bound these eighteen years" (see Lk. 13:10-17).

An anesthesiologist, a member of the American Medical Association, said that when there is an illness that has with it depression, anxiety, or fear, it may be caused by, or associated with, the work of an evil spirit. He said that medicine will not cure such an illness, except for a short time, after which the symptoms will return again. In such cases, he says, the spirit must first be cast out; then the sick one can be made well. In the parts of the world where the worship of evil spirits is carried on continually, there is much depression-related illness, which medicine does not seem to cure.

Satan attacks all of us, but we are told to resist him and he will flee from us (Jas. 4:1). He will bring doubts and fears and oppression, that we are to reject. If we harbor sin, or if we open our lives through drugs or spiritualism, we give opportunity for a spirit to take hold of areas in our lives. Then, if that spirit is able, he will bring others with him, as probably happened to Mary Magdalene, who had seven spirits, and the demoniacs, whose evil spirits were legion. Complete possession comes when the demons are able to beat down the personality and take over the whole person to make him appear to be completely insane. But we can praise God that even the man of Gadara, who was possessed by a legion of demons ("legion" coming from the Latin term for a Roman division of 3,000 to 6,000 men), was completely delivered by Jesus.

When we receive Jesus Christ into our lives, God "has taken us out of the power of darkness and created a place for us in the kingdom of the Son that he loves, and in him, we gain our freedom, the forgiveness of our sins" (Col. 1:13-14). But now that we are in Christ's Kingdom, we are to prepare ourselves to set free those who have also been taken captive by satan. In order to do this, we must put on the armor of God, which is related to our everyday living; for that is where most of the battle is fought. Paul tells us to put on the belt of truth which then binds our conversation to the truth as we speak to one another, and the breastplate of moral uprightness, which is the bond of faithfulness, in the family circle. Wherever we walk, the good news of peace is to be like the shoes on our feet. Above all, we are to take the great shield of faith that will protect us from all the arrows of slander and discouragement that will be aimed at us. The helmet of salvation, which identifies us with the children of God, we put on our heads. We then wield the mighty sword with the Spirit-directed Word of God, and pray the Spirit-inspired prayer. This is our spiritual armor to be worn every day so we will not be defeated by conflicts and doubts in our homes, with our families, and at work. (See Ephesians 6:10-18.)

We are not only to put on the armor of God and resist the devil in our lives, but we are also to be prepared to set others free. Jesus gave His disciples "power and authority over all devils... " (Lk. 9:1b). Later, He sent out 72 disciples, about which Luke continues to tell us in chapter 10 of his Gospel:

The seventy-two came back rejoicing. "Lord," they said "even the devils submit to us when we use your name." He said to them, "I watched Satan fall like lightning from heaven. Yes, I have given you power to tread underfoot serpents and scorpions and the whole strength of the enemy; nothing shall ever hurt you. Yet do not rejoice that the spirits submit to you; rejoice rather that your names are written in heaven" (Luke 10:17-20).

Their occupation was not to be with devils, but that did not minimize the fact that they had a great victory over the enemy.

145

It was then that, filled with joy by the Holy Spirit, he said, "I bless you, Father, Lord of heaven and of earth, for hiding these things from the learned and the clever and revealing them to mere children…. Happy the eyes that see what you see, for I tell you that many prophets and kings wanted to see what you see, and never saw it; to hear what you hear, and never heard it" (Luke 10:21,23b-24).

This victory over satan brought great joy to Jesus, for He knew that many of satan's captives were being released from their bondage. We can enter into that joy, because Jesus' great commission after His resurrection was based on the full authority in Heaven and earth that had been given to Him.

Because the Christian knows that he has power over evil spirits, there is a danger of seeking to exorcise where exorcism is not needed. If we try to cast out an evil spirit where there is none, we may instill fear in the person for whom we pray and dishonor the name of the Lord by our insistence. Therefore, the gift of discernment is given by the Holy Spirit, as He sees it is needed. Through this discernment, we become aware if an evil spirit is troubling a person, and perhaps even what kind of spirit it is.

Early in my ministry, a man asked if my wife and I would seek to help his wife. She had been in a mental hospital before, and then released. Her condition was worse now, but he was reluctant to see his wife suffer there again. My sister, who had seen the power of evil spirits in China, discerned the presence of satanic power. We took the woman into our home (which one should never do without first claiming by faith the protection of the Lord upon the home and family). My wife and I worked with her during the day, and my sister at night, for she seemed to be awake day and night. She could not read the Bible, even though she could read anything else. She would say things she would deeply regret; then we would pray with her. This went on for two exhausting weeks, for we did not know how to deal with the spirit. Finally, we invited some friends to help. We were standing around the piano singing some hymns about the blood of Christ, and she fell prostrate on the floor. We thought that she had fainted, but that was not so; instead, from that moment on, she was completely healthy in mind, and now for over 20 years, she has not had a recurrence of her mental problem. We had much to learn, and are still learning, but without the gift of discernment that woman might have had to suffer much in mental hospitals.

If we are called upon to help someone who is bound by satan, we must first protect ourselves. We must confess all our sins to God and accept His forgiveness, for the only hold that satan has on us is through unconfessed sin in our lives. Of this it is written, "We know that anyone who has been begotten by God does not sin, because the begotten Son of God protects him, and the Evil One does not touch him" (1 Jn. 5:18). John here is speaking of the Christian who does not live in sin: Here the word "touch," Strong says, means "to attach oneself to." So another reading would be, "No one who has become part of God's family makes a practice of sinning, for Christ, God's Son, holds him securely, and the devil cannot get his hands on him." This is a great encouragement. Symbolically, we speak of our protection "under His blood," for it means that we are trusting in His blood, shed in His death, by which He set us free from our sins. We use the symbol of the cross, for it speaks of the place and manner of His suffering for us.

These are scriptural symbols, but their value lies in our trust in the One who is symbolized in His sacrifice for us, not in the symbols themselves. Let us not make these sacred symbols become magic incantations, but let us use them to represent what we believe with our whole hearts, and by faith enter into the protection that God has given us there. Even the devils will know whether they are used in faith or not.

When we have taken our place of safety in Christ and accepted it in faith for the whole household, especially for the children, who should not be present when we pray for deliverance if it can be avoided, then we proceed by trusting the discernment that the Holy Spirit gives us. He may give it to us or to someone in our company involved in prayer, and our hearts will respond with peace when it is of God. Then, we must address the spirit directly in the name of Jesus and command him to leave, for this is an exercise of the authority Jesus gives us, not something He does for us.

As the Spirit of God leads us, so we must speak and, as we believe, the spirits must obey. There may indeed be a struggle at times, as there was when Jesus, after returning from the Mount of Transfiguration, healed the boy. But the authority is ours, and we must act upon it. We will continually need to listen to the Holy Spirit's direction, for the enemy is subtle and his warfare is just as unpredictable in the spiritual realm as it is in the material realm.

One afternoon, we met and had lunch with a young woman in another country. She had not only trusted in Christ as her Savior, but she had committed her whole life to Him, inviting the Holy Spirit to fill her. She was delighted that afternoon to receive more teaching, but I could see that she was so agitated that she could not even sit through the meal. After lunch, we parted. Then, before the day was over, we were called to help. When we came, she was violent and began throwing things, threatening us if we came near. Someone, with more understanding than mine, believingly said that they (i.e., the spirits) could not hurt us and commanded the spirit of murder to come out. Whereupon she replied—and yet not she, but the evil spirit speaking through her—"You think that there is only one of us; there are many of us in here." It was a fearful experience, but immediately, God gave peace as we believed. I then commanded the spirits to be quiet and to identify themselves. Some would name themselves through the woman, and some we named as we were impressed by the Spirit of God, bringing from her a response like, "How did you know that?" or, "There goes another one." We took authority over each one and commanded it to go and not return. Finally, it seemed that all, perhaps a dozen or more, were gone, and the woman collapsed. We laid hands on her, prayed for her, and then took her to her room. As soon as she entered her room, she was aware of another spirit's presence. We took authority over that one and cast it out too, and she was at peace. We then prayed that the Holy Spirit would fill all the areas formerly occupied by these spirits.

Later, I asked if it was she who was speaking in response to our command. She said that it surely was not. She knew that she had been a Christian for some time, but she had come from a very troubled home where these spirits evidently entered her. When she invited the Holy Spirit to fill her, she was aware of the evil forces within and had tried to cast them out, but was unable to do so. She has been free and filled with the joy of the Lord since the day of her deliverance.

Reference is sometimes made to binding a spirit, which refers to taking authority over the spirit so that it cannot go where it may want to go when it is cast out of the person. This act is very important, lest the spirit that is cast out enter into another person. Jesus exercised that authority, telling the spirits to keep silent, or giving them permission to do what He wished them to do.

When the person through whom the evil spirit is manifesting itself does not want to be freed from its power, then we may not be able to cast it out; however, we may be able to bind that spirit within him. While speaking at a Sunday worship service in Asia, a little boy, perhaps three or four years old, was disturbing the service by his very rebellious acts. If someone interfered with him, he would spit in that person's face, which, because of the people's custom of sitting on the floor, was rather convenient for him. My wife was quite upset with him until she discerned that the real problem was not the boy, but the spirit troubling him. She silently took authority over the spirit and instantly the boy was quiet and remained so during the service.

Later we discerned that an idol in the home was related to the trouble. When the idol was destroyed, the boy also was set free, and the report I received later was that he was a changed lad. In this case, the spirit had been bound within the boy during the service, but the ancestors' spirits, which were worshipped in the home, continued to trouble the boy until the idol was removed from the home.

When we have occasion to cast out an evil spirit from an area of a person's life, it is important that we ask the

Holy Spirit to come and fill this area. If it is left empty, it is like a vacuum that seeks to be filled. Jesus said:

When an unclean spirit goes out of a man it wanders through waterless country looking for a place to rest, and not finding one it says, "I will go back to the home I came from." But on arrival, finding it swept and tidied, it then goes off and brings seven other spirits more wicked than itself, and they go in and set up house there, so that the man ends up by being worse than he was before (Luke 11:24-26).

Therefore, it is most important that the Holy Spirit be invited to occupy the area of the life that the evil spirits held under their control. Healing of the memories and emotions may often be needed for such a wounded soul, and he will need the encouraging help of others.

In the whole spiritual realm, we need to realize that we are not fighting against the people, but against the powers of darkness who are troubling them. Mrs. Olivia Henry, a black Baptist pastor of Philadelphia, has set an example for many of us. It is said that during the Philadelphia riots in the 1960s, she sent her people out around the riot area and took authority over the evil forces that caused the people to hate each other. In this way, they quieted the area around her church. It is so important to love the person under the control of the evil spirits while we take decisive action against the spirits.

May we learn to fight in the spiritual warfare with a spiritual armor and spiritual weapons with the love of God in our hearts, rescue these taken captive by satan, and bring them to freedom in Jesus Christ.

As children of God, we need not be afraid of satan nor his evil powers. A friend from South America told a delightful story illustrating the authority that is ours in Christ.

She said that in the country where she lived a religion that worked through satanic powers was rampant. One day, the promoters of that religion decided to demonstrate through the means of a television program that their religion was greater in power than all others. For the occasion, they enlisted 200 mediums to take part in their demonstration. They also invited three clergymen. At the beginning of the hour's program, they told what they were going to do through their powers. Then, they invited the clergymen each to speak briefly. The words of the first two were quite ineffective, but the third man, a national pastor, took authority over all powers of the enemy in the name of Jesus. From that moment on, the forces of satan were bound, so that those who were going to show his power could do absolutely none of the things they had boasted of, although they had 200 mediums to help them.

I believe the day of challenge has come. We need to be armed with the power of God and let all know that the Kingdom of God is indeed come near.

Questions for Discussion

1. What did God tell Israel to avoid that opens the life to demonic powers? How can we discern whether a spiritual manifestation is from God or a counterfeit from satan?

2. How is the battle over satan and his demonic powers won? What is our armor to protect ourselves?

3. What preparation is necessary to have the authority to cast out evil spirits?

Chapter 8

The Gifts of Tongues, Prophecy, and Interpretation

Of all the gifts of the Holy Spirit, none is so much feared as the gift of tongues. This is understandable in our rationalistic society. Yet, how can we rationally explain conversion, prayer, or the sense of the presence of God in worship? As soon as we attempt to, we find that we are already reaching beyond the bounds of reason. The worship of God comes from a higher dimension than man's sense of reason can attain. Perhaps preserving the sanity of our speech is the last resort of reason.

The effects of a materialistic philosophy, limiting valid knowledge to our five senses and reason, have expelled much of the supernatural in the Christianity of the West. Eastern Orthodox Christianity, integrating this philosophy in a more subtle world view, has accepted the exercise of supernatural gifts—specifically, the gift of tongues, up to the present day. From the beginning, speaking in tongues was part of the Church's expression of worship. Therefore, let us allow God to continue to express Himself through us as He wills, and not seek to bind Him by our rationalistic philosophies.

We will consider the gifts of prophecy, tongues, and their interpretation together following the precedent set by the apostle Paul in the fourteenth chapter of First Corinthians. There we see that the gift of tongues is primarily for the private building up of the believer. We need to look clearly at what Paul has to say to us in order that we neither exaggerate, nor minimize, the gifts that the Holy Spirit wants to give to the Church.

When we look carefully at the ministry of the prophet and the gift of prophecy, we see that they are basically the same in the Old and New Testaments. The Old Testament prophet received many of his messages from God through dreams and visions (see Num. 12:6); and in the New Testament, Peter associates prophecy with dreams and visions when the Holy Spirit comes (see Acts 2:12).

The prophet in the Old Testament became a sign to Israel that God was faithful and would perform His word. Thus Elijah, in the time of Israel's turning from God to false prophets, proved that God was still the living God who heard and answered prayer. Isaiah was made to be a sign to Ahaz because the king would not ask for the sign that God wanted to give him. Therefore, God told Isaiah to make an announcement of his son's birth before he was conceived, which would be a sign that God would defeat the enemies. Daniel, too, became a sign of the God of Israel's power in the midst of the heathen nations.

The prophets have a place in the New Testament Church as personal gifts from the risen Christ. "And to some, his gift was that they should be apostles; to some, prophets; to some, evangelists; to some, pastors and teachers; so that the saints together make a unity in the work of service, building up the body of Christ" (Eph. 4:11-12). These prophets play a vital role in the Church after Pentecost, as their function is to carry a special message from God. Agabus, from the church of Antioch, predicts a famine, whereupon the church, recognizing the voice of God through the prophet, prepares relief for the Christians in Judea (see Acts 11:27-30). The same prophet later warns Paul of his imprisonment if he goes to Jerusalem (see Acts 27:10-11). It is, evidently, through the prophets in Antioch that the Holy Spirit tells the Church to send out Paul and Barnabas on their missionary journey (see Acts 13). Finally, the greatest prophet of them all, the apostle John, is given the series of visions about the future of the Church.

However, the chief ministry of the prophet is not to tell the future, but to teach and encourage God's people; this is evident in the messages of the prophets. Paul tells us specifically what the message of prophecy is: "...the man who prophesies does talk to other people, to their improvement, their encouragement, and their consolation" (1 Cor. 14:3). He goes on to say that prophecy is given to build up and instruct the Church. I now know that we had a prophet in the church in my early ministry as a pastor. This layman would come to me on Monday morning to encourage and exhort me (as he would do among all the members of the church) in real love. However, we did not recognize that as a gift of prophecy.

There is another area of ministry wherein some of us have neglected the gift of prophecy, to our great loss. It is in the ordination of men and women to various forms of spiritual ministry. Paul says to his young disciple Timothy, "You have in you a spiritual gift which was given to you when the prophets spoke and the body of elders laid their hands on you; do not let it lie unused" (1 Tim. 4:14).

When Paul is traveling through Lystra and Derbe, on his second missionary journey, he finds Timothy, who is well spoken of by the Christians. He wants to have Timothy with him, so in preparation for that ministry, Paul and the elders of the church lay their hands on him. As they do so, God gives a word of prophecy concerning Timothy, which says that he will receive a spiritual gift. When Paul later writes to Timothy from his prison cell, he calls upon him not to neglect the gift that was given to him by the word of prophecy. This indicates that the word of prophecy is not automatically fulfilled, but operates on the basis of the principles laid down in the Old Testament.

> *On occasion, I decree for some nation, for some kingdom, that I will tear up, knock down, destroy; but if this nation, against which I have pronounced sentence, abandons its wickedness, I then change my mind about the evil which I had intended to inflict on it. On another occasion, I decree for some nation, for some kingdom, that I will build up and plant; but if that nation does what displeases me, refusing to listen to my voice, I then change my mind about the good which I had intended to confer on it* (Jeremiah 18:7-10).

If a word of warning is given by the prophet and it is heeded, then the judgment will not take place, as in the case of God's warning to Nineveh through Jonah. If a promise is given, but it is not believed, then it will not be fulfilled. It is on this principle that Paul is speaking to his young follower. Timothy, evidently, has been neglecting the gift that was given through the work of prophecy, and it might be lost. In fact, later Timothy is still not exercising it as Paul wishes. So in his second letter, he asks Timothy to stir into flame the gift that is within him, given through the laying on of hands (see 2 Tim. 16). Thus, the gift of prophecy plays a vital part in the ordination to the ministry in the Church.

I have seen this beautifully in operation in a local church. The pastors and elders had been waiting upon God for direction concerning requests for the laying on of hands in prayer for further ministry. Accordingly, as God led them, the elders called the candidates for ordination to receive the laying on of hands. As the pastors and elders prayed and waited upon God, He gave them words of prophecy concerning the candidates. There were words of direction, or of warning, or encouragement, that were very helpful in guiding each candidate to his future ministry. There were also promises of specific gifts of the Spirit that were to be received and acted upon. With this laying on of hands, and these words of prophecy, came some encouraging results that I was able to see!

The word of prophecy is to be tested by the church. Paul says, "As for prophets, let two or three of them speak, and the others attend to them" (1 Cor. 14:29). Even concerning the prophecy of Scripture, we read: "At the same time, we must be most careful to remember that the interpretation of scriptural prophecy is never a matter for the individual. Why? Because no prophecy ever came from man's initiative. When men spoke for God it was the Holy Spirit that moved them" (2 Pet. 1:20-21).

The word of prophecy today is not on the same plane as the prophecy of Scripture, but it comes from the same Spirit. We know that Paul wrote other letters that are not part of the New Testament, and evidently he was guided by the Holy Spirit in writing them, too. However, God chose to preserve certain writings to form what we call the Scriptures, as God's message to the world. Our word of prophecy should come from the Holy Spirit also, and as a consequence, it will be true and valid for the occasion. However, it is not put on the same level as Scripture since it is not part of that universal message, the Word of God, but instead, it must be tested by that very Scripture and by the Holy Spirit, who both inspired it and now lives in us.

It is this gift of prophecy that makes the message of God alive to the Church today. For by the gift of prophecy, the Holy Spirit takes the general principles of the Scriptures and makes them relevant to the immediate situation. Thus, when Elijah, the prophet, evidently read the warning of Scripture (see Lev. 26:18-19) that if Israel sinned, God would make the heavens like brass and so withhold the rain, Elijah, led by the Holy Spirit, applied this warning to the immediate occasion. The Spirit apparently impressed upon him that the very Scripture, which he had read, applied at this very time to King Ahab. So, he went to the king and said that it would not rain except by his own word, and so it did not rain for three years and six months.

The world needs to know today, as then, that God is alive and speaks to us concerning our present-day problems and needs. The word of prophecy is not usually something strange or far off, but it is something immediately relevant to a particular occasion today. Take, for instance, the word that came to a church in a Sunday morning worship service, which, in essence, was: "You are in too much of a hurry. You must be quiet and wait upon Me, so that you can hear what I have to say," and again, "I am pouring out My blessing today. Come and drink and let your soul be satisfied."

These were words of exhortation and encouragement for that very service. Of course, pride or self-love can enter such a word of prophecy and mar it, as it also can mar preaching, but the church that is listening to the Spirit will learn to recognize the Spirit's voice. His prophecy will edify and build up the church. We need the Word of God as a sure guide for our lives, but we need, also, today's word of prophecy to make the Scriptures relevant to our immediate needs. However, I believe the time is at hand when God is again giving greater prophecies that may even refer to nations.

In examining the gift of tongues, let us look carefully at what the Scriptures say concerning it. As we let the light of God shine into this area of Christian experience, where so much fear and confusion has existed, we will see that this gift, too, is good, as are all the gifts of God. The demonstration and exercise of the gift of tongues is described in the Book of Acts; the explanation of this gift is given in First Corinthians. Since St. Paul compares the exercise of the gifts of prophecy and of tongues in First Corinthians 14, we need but put his words into two parallel columns: in one, what he says about prophecy; in the other, what he says about tongues. We are aware that Paul is differentiating the exercise of the gift of prophecy from the gift of tongues in this chapter.

However, it is also valid to look separately at what he says concerning each gift. Inasmuch as we have briefly looked at prophecy, let us now look at what St. Paul teaches us by the Spirit concerning the gift of tongues. In doing this, we may be surprised at the positive statements he makes concerning this gift. In this chapter, Paul speaks of three different aspects of tongues. First, the private prayer of the individual (see 1 Cor. 14:1-19); then, tongues as a sign to the world (1 Cor. 14:20-25); and finally, tongues in its public use (1 Cor 14:26-40).

Paul first describes the gift of tongues: "Anybody with the gift of tongues speaks to God, but not to other people; because nobody understands him when he talks in the spirit about mysterious things" (1 Cor. 14:2). (Here I object to the word "ecstasy" for "tongues," as used in one of the modern translations, for there is no indication anywhere in Scripture of tongues being called a language of ecstasy, i.e., a language expressing transport or rapture or delight. It is simply called "tongues.") The one speaking in tongues is speaking to God in a language not understood by man. We need first to accept this as God's explanation and not try to explain it away, as some have done with all that is miraculous. Since by tongues a man speaks mysteries in the Spirit, the language by which he speaks these mysteries is in the spiritual realm, and it is only by the Spirit of God that one can interpret such a (spiritual) language.

So much is made of the comment "If we cannot understand tongues, what good are they?" The answer is that even the gift of salvation is beyond our rational comprehension, but if it is grasped in faith we receive its benefits. Let us let God be sovereign. If He says that He has a gift for us which our mind cannot understand, then let us accept it as such, remembering that truth is not limited to the five senses and reason alone. The spiritual realm stands high above the rational.

Paul then tells us what the purpose of the gift of tongues is. "The one with the gift of tongues talks for his own benefit [edifies himself]" (1 Cor. 14:4). This is God's provision to build us up spiritually. Presumably, if we do not need edifying or being built up spiritually, then we do not need the gift of tongues, but who is that? However, the one who ministers to others' needs continually will find that he becomes exhausted, unless he can renew his spiritual strength. This, Paul says, is done by praying in tongues. Evidently, that is the reason he goes on to say, "I should like you all to have the gift of tongues" (1 Cor. 14:5), for he must have sensed they all needed it.

We do not, however, seek to minimize the words about prophecy, "The man who prophesies does so for the benefit of the community...I would much rather that you could prophesy" (1 Cor. 14:4b-5). Because prophecy edifies the church, we should seek it more for its public use. So it seems plain that Paul wished that all the Corinthians (and if the epistles are for us, then we are included) would speak in tongues privately and that they would prophesy publicly. Then he goes on to remind them (see 1 Cor. 14:5-12) that if this private gift is used publicly, without an interpreter, it is meaningless and becomes confusing. Therefore, we should seek this gift for its proper purpose, personal edification, and keep it in its proper place, in private prayer, unless there is an interpreter. For public ministry, let us rather seek the gift of prophecy.

We are not left to wonder what this kind of prayer really is. "For if I use this gift in my prayers, my spirit may be praying, but my mind is left barren" (1 Cor. 14:14). The mind or intellect, in this prayer, is inactive, so it is a prayer of the spirit and not of the mind. We remember that the way of communication from God to man is as follows: The word or thought originates with the Father, is revealed through the Son, and is interpreted or applied to us by the Holy Spirit.

Contact with us comes as God's Holy Spirit awakens our spirit; then our spirit moves upon our soul, and our soul upon our body. Speaking in tongues is the communication of our spirit with God's Spirit, without making use of our mind. This is similar to what we do as we worship God and know that we have been in His presence, though we cannot explain it rationally. The gift of tongues is irrational, i.e., above reason, but that does not make it invalid: for it is spiritual and the spiritual realm is different from the rational. In this case, even the body cooperates without the mind, for the tongue speaks the word that the spirit desires.

The natural question that comes to us is, "What is the use of speaking in tongues if we cannot even understand what we are saying?" The best illustration to me of its value is in the experience of Rev. William C. Nelson, pastor and former editor in the American Baptist Convention. He told this story to a small group of us who were interested, but had questions about praying in tongues.

After this fine pastor had opened his life to the Spirit of God and received the gift of tongues, he exercised it privately, not even telling his wife about his experience for about a year. One night, however, he received a call from a nurse in a hospital; one of the young girls from his church had been in a serious automobile accident. He found the girl in such a critical condition that the nurses had not even dared to undress or move her. He asked the family to step out of the room, and as he stood by the bedside, he wondered what he should pray for. If he prayed that she be healed, his mind told him that she might be nothing but a "living vegetable." He thought of praying that she might die peacefully, but then how could he pray that a 17-year-old girl die? Then it occurred to him to pray in the spirit. He did so for about 20 minutes, as the nurse went in and out caring for the girl. When he went out, he said to the family, "She'll be all right." But as he stepped into the elevator he thought, "What did I say? She'll be all right?" This was beyond what reason could accept. But after three months, the girl was back in school and the specialist was so impressed that he asked Bill to pray for others in serious conditions. As Bill told of this, he related his prayer in tongues to the words of Paul:

In the same way, the Spirit helps us in our weakness. We do not know what we ought to pray for, but the Spirit himself intercedes for us with groans that words cannot express. And he who searches our hearts knows the mind of the Spirit, because the Spirit intercedes for the saints in accordance with God's will (Romans 8:26-27, NIV).

Pastor Nelson's mind had told him that the girl could not be fully healed, but his spirit heard the prayer of the Holy Spirit (from whom all prayer really originates), and in the spirit, he prayed that prayer and was heard. As he went out of the hospital room, he said what he had just caught from his spirit, "She'll be all right," but then his

163

mind immediately wanted to take over with rational thinking and doubt it.

So praying in tongues lifts us beyond rational thought and is the expression of the desires of the Spirit of God. That is why it brings such praise to God spontaneously, why it hits the target so effectively, and why it is such a power against spiritual forces.

However, the Spirit of God also directs our mind through rational thought in prayer. So, Paul says he will allow his spirit to pray one kind of prayer, and his mind to pray another. He indicates that both kinds of prayer are valid and he would exercise both. The use of praying in tongues for public worship may be measured by these words: "When I am in the presence of the community, I would rather say five words that mean something than ten thousands words in a tongue" (1 Cor. 14:19). However, its value for private prayer is measured also by Paul's words in verse 18, "I thank God that I have a greater gift of tongues than all of you," and again, "I should like you all to have the gift of tongues" (1 Cor. 14:5).

We must also take note that Paul's words in Romans 8:28, so familiarly quoted but sometimes in false resignation, "We know that by turning everything to their good God co-operates with all those who love him, with all those that he has called according to his purpose," follow his words about prayer that is directed by the Spirit, even in inarticulate groans. The implication is that if we pray the Spirit's prayer, then God will make all things work together for good to them that love Him. We also note that in spiritual warfare Paul tells us to pray in the Spirit (see Eph. 6:18), for our prayer may be very poorly directed by the mind, but needs to be directed by the Spirit of God.

164

Then Paul goes on to say that there are two kinds of singing: "For if I use this gift in my prayers, my spirit may be praying but my mind is left barren...And sing praises not only with the spirit but the mind as well?" (1 Cor. 14:14-15). Perhaps, this is what he is referring to when he speaks about singing hymns and spiritual songs (see Eph. 5:19; Col. 3:16). So singing in the Spirit becomes part of spiritual worship. It is amazing to hear a large congregation of people singing in the Spirit. The impression of many is that, at first, the singing sounds as if an orchestra is tuning up, then it swells into a harmony of praise, and finally it diminishes to perfect silence without an outward signal from anyone. It is said that the chant in liturgical church worship is a carryover from the singing in the Spirit of past times.

We often hear that tongues are a sign of the baptism of the Holy Spirit. It is perfectly true that they are one of the gifts of the Spirit. However, I do not believe we are ever told to look for tongues as an evidence of the fullness of the Holy Spirit. (We will see later what Jesus clearly indicates should be an evidence of the baptism of the Spirit.) However, Paul tells us tongues are a sign to the unbeliever.

*In the written Law it says: **Through men speaking strange languages and through the lips of foreigners, I shall talk to the nation, and still they will not listen to me, says the Lord.** You see then, that the strange languages are meant to be a sign not for believers but for unbelievers...* (1 Corinthians 14:21-22).

This happened at Pentecost, the first time that tongues was given. As the disciples were waiting for the fulfillment of Jesus' promise:

They were all filled with the Holy Spirit, and began to speak foreign languages as the Spirit gave them the gift of speech. Now there were devout men living in Jerusalem from every nation under heaven, and at this sound they all assembled, each one bewildered to hear these men speaking his own language. They were amazed and astonished. "Surely," they said, "all these men speaking are Galileans? How does it happen that each of us hears them in his own native language? Parthians, Medes and Elamites; people from Mesopotamia, Judaea and Cappadocia, Pontus and Asia, Phrygia and Pamphylia, Egypt and the parts of Libya around Cyrene; as well as visitors from Rome–Jews and proselytes alike–Cretans and Arabs; we hear them preaching in our own language about the marvels of God." Everyone was amazed and unable to explain it; they asked one another what it all meant (Acts 2:4-12).

These words of praise to God were understood by the people from various countries, as the disciples spoke in their language. They were, therefore, signs of the power of God upon them.

Recently, a woman went to a friend for counsel. The friend, feeling unable to help her, began to pray in tongues. When she finished, the needy woman told her friend that she had answered all her questions, and that she was amazed that her friend's prayers had been spoken not only in the Iranian language, but the aristocratic Iranian, for she knew that her praying friend was totally unfamiliar with the language of Iran.

Though such experiences are far from the usual, they are a sign to the one who hears them. The hearer is astonished by the ability of the other to speak his language;

but through the process, he receives a message from God. A friend from India has received not only temporary, but permanent languages to speak to people to whom he was sent. When the language in "tongues" is understood by another, then we are told that tongues are a sign to the unbeliever.

The public use of the gift of tongues and the interpretation of the same are both gifts of the Holy Spirit. They go hand in hand; where the one is, there the other will be also. There is a difference between the private exercise of the gift of tongues, which is for personal edification (see 1 Cor. 14:4), and the message of tongues to the church with interpretation, which is for the edification of the church and is equal to prophecy (1 Cor. 14:5b). It seems that the gift of tongues is for all, for how could Paul say, "I should like you all to have the gift of tongues," if that were not so? It seems that all the believers at Pentecost and all of Cornelius' household (see Acts 10) spoke in tongues. However, the public exercise of that gift, which is equal to prophecy, may not be for all, as is suggested by Paul's questions.

In the Church, God has given the first place to apostles, the second to prophets, the third to teachers; after them, miracles, and after them the gift of healing; helpers, good leaders, those with many languages. Are all of them apostles, or all of them prophets, or all of them teachers? Do they all have the gift of miracles, or all have the gift of healing? Do all speak strange languages, and all interpret them? (1 Corinthians 12:28-30)

The obvious answer to these questions is no. The public expression is limited. "If there are people present with

167

the gift of tongues, let only two or three, at the most, be allowed to use it, and only one at a time, and there must be someone to interpret. If there is no interpreter present, they must keep quiet in the church and speak only to themselves and to God" (1 Cor. 14:27-28). We note that since the speaker is to stop speaking if there is not an interpreter, and to start in private again, that he is in control of himself. He can start when he wants and stop when he wants."Prophets can always control their prophetic spirits" (1 Cor. 14:32). So it is also with the one who speaks in tongues.

We are told that one manifest difference between the one who speaks in tongues by the Holy Spirit and one who does so by satanic influence (as in places where satan worship is prevalent) is that the Holy Spirit always allows us our free will, and we are in control of ourselves. The one speaking under satan's power is in a trance, or at least not in control of himself. God never violates our free will, but desires us to yield to Him voluntarily.

When the gifts of the Spirit are manifest in a church, there must be discipline, for the Holy Spirit is one who brings order wherever He is in control. All must be done to build up the church. Nevertheless, while there is discipline, note that it is not judgment. The one speaking in tongues, where there is no interpreter, is not told that what he spoke is of the devil, but rather to continue to speak to himself and to God at home.

I saw a demonstration of this in an informal church meeting where a lay member of the church was presiding. In the course of the meeting, a woman spoke out with much enthusiasm in tongues. The leader of the meeting waited for an interpretation, but when there was none, he went on with the meeting. Something seemed wrong, but in a moment the pastor spoke up, addressing the woman and those in attendance, saying that the words she had spoken were not for the congregation, for if they had been there would have been an interpreter. But the woman said that she felt so full of praise and joy that she needed to express it. The pastor acknowledged that, but said kindly that after a while, she would learn to know the difference between a word in tongues which was for the congregation, and one that was for her private worship. Thus wisely, firmly, and yet with much love, correction was given to one new in her Christian experience.

This is the pattern that Paul gives us. When we act with such love toward each other, we will not need to forbid the speaking in tongues (1 Cor. 14:39). This gift will become a blessing to the church, as it will bring a fresh message from God at the proper time and place.

We have recognized that some seek the gift of tongues above all other gifts and from impure motives, while others stay away because of prejudice. God will never force this gift upon us. We must first be persuaded in our minds and hearts that this is indeed a gift of God, and therefore good. We may need to be persuaded of the promise of Jesus so that we will not need to be afraid that we will get a false gift or an imitation when we seek it from God.

What father among you would hand his son a stone when he asked for bread? Or hand him a snake instead of a fish? Or hand him a scorpion if he asked for an egg? If you then, who are evil, know how to give your children what is good, how much more will the heavenly Father give the Holy Spirit to those who ask him! (Luke 11:11-13)

When we believe that God will give us nothing but good, then we may dare to ask Him for this gift also. Some say, "If God wants to give me this gift, I will receive it, but I will not seek it." But if we took that attitude towards our salvation, we would not be saved. God does not give us His gifts unless we desire them. The manner in which He gives us this gift, as the manner in which He draws us to salvation, will vary with each person—some receive the gift of tongues suddenly, and the language will flow out, as from an artesian well; to many, however, it may come by one or two syllables at a time at first.

However, perhaps in our rational culture the greatest barrier is pride. For our holding out on tongues, as stated before, may be reason's last stand. We cannot defend tongues rationally, for it is not rational but spiritual. It is our pride that must give in, usually through the great hunger and thirst that Jesus speaks of, before we will even dare to allow God to give us this gift. If our hunger is the famishing that Jesus speaks of in the Beatitudes, then we can respond to the slightest prompting of the Holy Spirit when He gives us just a syllable in prayer or even the slightest movement of the lips.

The most natural question that arises, when we receive either small promptings or a full flow of language, is whether it is really from God or whether one has produced it himself. One minister tested his experience with a few syllables for three years to see whether it was of self or from God. But he found that it came when his heart was clean, when he prayed and gave praise to God, and so finally he accepted it, and the language began to come so freely that he could pray and praise God in tongues for an hour or two at a time. It became a means of spiritual edification as he ministered to others, and his best preparation for both his studies and his teaching and preaching of the Word. Through this gift we may come nearest to the fulfillment of Paul's admonition, "Pray constantly" (1 Thess. 5:17).

The gift of tongues may be God's answer to the confusion of tongues at the tower of Babel. I asked a noted Christian psychologist, from Berlin, who is also an authority in music, what tongues are psychologically. She said that from early sources, she and others had learned that music was man's universal language (before Babel). When one speaks in tongues, his spirit brings forth language from that universal source; hence, the many languages, known and unknown, that are expressed by the gift of tongues. Whether by that means or not, we know that God still speaks supernaturally to, and through, people; and thus, the tongue that could have been set on fire by hell can be sanctified by the Holy Spirit. May we use every tongue to praise Him who is worthy of all our adoration and worship.

However, we know that satan seeks to counterfeit every gift of God. The African pastors, who had come out of witchcraft, confirmed that to me. When I asked them what works they had seen that might be compared to the gifts of the Holy Spirit, they mentioned healing, miracles, prophecy, tongues, interpretation of tongues, wisdom, faith, and knowledge. As I asked the same question of pastors of other areas, they would list the same eight manifestations. In fact, the one gift that satan did not, or could not, counterfeit was the gift of discernment of spirits. If he did, he would defeat himself.

Although these African pastors had seen eight of these gifts of the Holy Spirit counterfeited by satan, they did not doubt the reality of that power that God gives. On the contrary, after seeing the powers of the enemy in destructive works, they were very eager to know the real power of God through the Holy Spirit. When they then received the Spirit, the sick were healed and the captives set free to their great joy and amazement.

Some people have become discouraged because they have seen false powers. Certainly, we do not want any counterfeits in our ministry. However, where there is reality there are apt to be counterfeits, because satan is always at work. So let us be open before God so that He can examine our work and bring forth that which is real. We know that God's gifts are not to be neglected or ignored, but are good and will bring great blessing. May we not allow satan to frighten us away from the reality so that there is nothing even good enough to counterfeit.

Questions for Discussion

1. What is the primary purpose of the gift of prophecy?
2. Why is the gift of tongues so feared in our culture?
3. What are the three ways in which tongues are to be used?

Chapter 9

The Baptism With the Holy Spirit

Now that we have studied the gifts of the Holy Spirit, or ways by which the Holy Spirit wants to express himself, we must consider our response.

The way of mature discipleship is the way of the cross that leads to resurrection power. Jesus has promised power, and He will give it, while we stand amazed to see what God is doing. However, Jesus never hid the fact that it would be a costly way.

Then to all he said, "If anyone wants to be a follower of mine, let him renounce himself and take up his cross every day and follow me. For anyone who wants to save his life will lose it; but anyone who loses his life for my sake, that man will save it. What gain, then, is it for a man to have won the whole world and to have lost or ruined his very self? For if anyone is ashamed of me and of my words, of him the Son of Man will be ashamed when he comes in his own glory and in the glory of the Father and the holy angels (Luke 9:23-26).

I do not believe Jesus wants us to enter into great Christian experiences, or even discipleship, without first carefully counting the cost.

In preaching, the Spirit gives power that has a cutting edge. It has the foolishness of God with it that will easily be rejected by the wisdom of this world, and slandered by those who will not receive it. When Jesus preached His first sermon in His own hometown synagogue, the response indicated the Spirit's work. There was a stir of admiration at the beautiful words that He spoke, but when He made the application to His neighbors own lives, they became furiously angry. They drove Him out of town, and even wanted to push Him over the brink of the precipice of a hill nearby. There was a combination of the beauty that attracts one to the truth; and the purifying fire that separates one from all superficial religion. There is healing, but through the burning out of all that is evil. This fire of the Spirit does not easily attract great crowds. We read:

Great crowds accompanied him on his way and he turned and spoke to them, "If any man comes to me without hating his father, mother, wife, children, brothers, sisters, yes and his own life too, he cannot be my disciple. Anyone who does not carry his cross and come after me cannot be my disciple. And indeed, which of you here, intending to build a tower, would not first sit down and work out the cost to see if he had enough to complete it? Otherwise, if he laid the foundation and then found himself unable to finish the work, the onlookers would all start making fun of him and saying, 'Here is a man who started to build and was unable to finish.' Or again, what king marching to war against another king would not first sit down and consider whether with ten thousand men he could stand up to the other who advanced against him with twenty thousand? If not, then while the other king was still a long way off, he would send envoys to sue for peace. So in the same way, none of you can be my disciple unless he gives up all his possessions" (Luke 14:25-33).

Let us count the cost of discipleship before we ask for the authority that attends it.

The power of the Holy Spirit is a real power; therefore, it is necessary that we cleanse ourselves of all evil. It is especially important that we confess any involvement with the occult powers that presume to give direction or spiritual illumination apart from Jesus Christ, the Son of God. We do not want or need to become legalistic, but we want to be clean. We need to ask the Holy Spirit to point out any area in which we may be in bondage to evil spirit powers, through fortunetelling, the ouija board, the horoscope, drugs that open the unconscious to spirit powers, spiritualism, and through all that is contrary to the Word of God. These things need to be confessed to God and forgiven; the devil needs to be renounced. We are dealing with real powers, the powers of satan and the powers of God. If we do not cleanse ourselves of the powers of darkness before we invite the powers of light, confusion results. Therefore, we need to renounce the devil and his works, and then open our lives to the Holy Spirit to take over our whole being.

We need to ask both for the cleansing from all evil and for the love of God to fill our hearts, so that it can be a saving accompaniment to all the gifts of the Spirit. The apostle Paul says, "What the Spirit brings is very different (from the works of the flesh): love, joy, peace, patience, kindness, goodness, trustfulness, gentleness and self-control" (Gal. 5:22). These all may be summed up in love. This love, the fruit of the Spirit, should never be separated from the gifts of the Spirit; the fruit refers to *being*, the gifts to *doing*. They must work together; love must attend the gifts of the Spirit.

The great chapter of love, First Corinthians 13, is found in the midst of Paul's explanation of the gifts of the Spirit. He says that the gifts of tongues, prophecy, knowledge, and faith are empty, powerless, and vain if they are not related to love. So he points out the necessity of love.

If ever a church needs love, it does so when the gifts of the Spirit become manifest. Love is patient with others when they are blessed and we are not, and love will not allow jealousy to creep in. It is not boastful when God uses us, even to perform a miracle, and it is not rude to others who are not greatly gifted. It does not insist on its own way when a word of knowledge has come, but trusts God to perform His purpose through the church. It does not become irritable or resentful towards others who do not understand. It is not happy over the fall of another, but rejoices when right prevails. Love bears all things, even the slander of others, and it believes in all that God sees in the other person; it hopes, and therefore patiently waits, for the fulfillment of God's promises, and endures all the ups and downs of public opinion.

A great measure of such love is needed when the Spirit gives His gifts as He wills and chooses to use us according to His wisdom. As someone has said, "St. Peter was filled with the Spirit and received 3,000 souls, and St. Stephen was filled with the Spirit and received 3,000 stones." Love, however, has no fear, for it trusts God completely. Therefore, when these temporary gifts of the Spirit are imbued with and directed by love, they gain an eternal quality; without love, they lose what they have. Let us, therefore, seek much love along with the fullness of the Holy Spirit.

"You will be baptized with the Holy Spirit" is a Scriptural term, perhaps used more frequently than any other, but it is not the only one used in the New Testament. John the Baptist, in introducing Jesus, spoke of the comparative roles of Jesus and himself. John baptized with water, a baptism leading people to repentance; Jesus would baptize with the Holy Spirit, a purifying fire separating the grain from the chaff (see Mt. 3:11-12). Jesus reminds His followers of this when He says, "Wait there for what the Father had promised. 'It is,' he had said, 'what you have heard me speak about: John baptized with water but you, not many days from now, will be baptized with the Holy Spirit' " (see Acts 1:4b-5). He also says, in Luke 24:49, that they are to be endued, or clothed, or armed with power from on high. Then, when the Holy Spirit did come upon them at Pentecost, Luke says, "They were all filled with the Holy Spirit" (see Acts 2:4a). Thus, filling is a correct term, as long as we do not put our limitations upon it. When they were filled, the gifts of the Spirit immediately began to manifest themselves through them. Peter speaks of this fullness as a gift that is poured out upon them (see Acts 10:44), perhaps similar to the ointment poured out upon Jesus by Mary, and so it is an anointing of the Spirit. So the terms "the baptism with the Holy Spirit," "the empowering," "the filling," and "the anointing" all speak of various aspects of the same experience.

After Jesus had told His followers how important it was for them to stay in Jerusalem until the Holy Spirit had come upon them, He described to them the purpose of the baptism with the Holy Spirit. He said that they would receive power to witness for Him effectively. "But you will receive power when the Holy Spirit comes on you, and then you will be my witnesses not only in Jerusalem but throughout Judaea and Samaria, and indeed to the ends of the earth" (Acts 1:8). This describes exactly what happened to the early church, for they received such power that men feared that they would "turn the world upside down."

As we look at the record of the early church, we are not particularly impressed that they spoke with tongues, though they did that. What impresses us is that the power of God was so evidently with them. This has ever been so.

R.A. Torrey, the second president of the Moody Bible Institute, who with Dwight L. Moody led hundreds of ministers into the baptism with the Holy Spirit, describes at length that experience, and its necessity for Christian testimony and service. "The Baptism with the Holy Spirit is the Spirit of God coming upon the believer, filling his mind with a real apprehension of truth, and taking possession of his faculties, imparting to him gifts not otherwise his, but which qualify him for the service to which God has called him."!1.

As Jesus said, the baptism with the Holy Spirit has to do with power for our witness for Christ in whatever situation of life we may be. So this experience is not primarily a doctrinal one, but a practical one. If we are not able to make

1.   R.A. Torrey, *What the Bible Teaches* (NY: Revell, 1898), 276.

our witness for Christ effective, then we need to open our lives to the Holy Spirit for empowering. It is not a question of having the Holy Spirit, for if we are children of God, we have the Holy Spirit (see Rom. 8:9). Dr. Torrey goes on to say, "It is one thing to have the Holy Spirit dwelling way back of consciousness in some hidden sanctuary of the being and something quite different, and vastly more, to have Him take possession of the whole House that He inhabits."[2]

Therefore, we need to surrender ourselves very specifically to the Holy Spirit in order that He may manifest His power in any way that He chooses.

> The Baptism with the Holy Spirit is an operation of the Holy Spirit distinct from and subsequent and additional to His regenerating work. A man may be regenerated by the Holy Spirit and still not be baptized with the Holy Spirit. In regeneration there is an impartation of life, and the one who received it is saved; in the Baptism with the Holy Spirit there is an impartation of power and the one who receives it is fitted for service.[3]

We will know that we have had the baptism of the Holy Spirit, not necessarily through the experience which attends its coming, but by the evidence of new power in our lives. Often, as we look back upon our recent experiences, we will recognize that this power has come. In retrospect, we will see how in any one or all of the gifts the Spirit has manifested himself.

---

2. R.A. Torrey, *What the Bible Teaches* (NY: Revell, 1910), 178.
3. R.A. Torrey, *What the Bible Teaches*, 271.

However, we must not confuse the *signs* that may attend the coming of the Holy Spirit with *that one thing* that Jesus said we would receive following the baptism with the Holy Spirit.

> *When Pentecost day came round, they had all met in one room, when suddenly they heard what sounded like a powerful wind from heaven, the noise of which filled the entire house in which they were sitting; and something appeared to them that seemed like tongues of fire; these separated and came to rest on the head of each of them. They were all filled with the Holy Spirit, and began to speak foreign languages as the Spirit gave them the gift of speech* (Acts 2:1-4).

Noise like a wind and flames of fire have appeared at other times in the history of the church when the Holy Spirit came in power. When the threatened disciples prayed for new power "...to heal and to work miracles and marvels through the name of your holy servant Jesus...the house where they were assembled rocked; they were all filled with the Holy Spirit and began to proclaim the word of God boldly" (Acts 4:30-31). And yet, we are not told to look for an earthquake when the Spirit comes.

At the home of Cornelius, the Roman officer, the Spirit came upon the Gentiles, who were gathered to hear what Peter had to say, and they spoke in tongues and praised God (see Acts 10). At Ephesus, St. Paul laid his hands on a small group and they spoke with tongues and prophesied (see Acts 19). All of these things and other signs have accompanied the coming of the Holy Spirit upon people, yet Jesus did not tell us to look for any of these signs. In Mark's Gospel, we read: "These are the signs that will be associated with the believers: in my name they will cast out devils; they will have the gift of tongues; they will pick up snakes in their hands, and be unharmed should they drink deadly poison; they will lay their hands on the sick, who will recover" (Mk. 16:17-18).

Yet we cannot take any one of these to be the initial sign of the baptism of the Holy Spirit. If we did, we should have to take them all. Any of these may follow the Spirit's working through our lives, but we are not told to look for any of them. Let God send such signs when, and as, He will. What Jesus did promise was power to be His witnesses. This is what we should look for, whether any or all of the other "signs" become evident. Of what value is a great experience accompanying the baptism with the Holy Spirit if the result is not power to witness to Jesus? And what matters whether other signs accompany the experience or not, as long as the power of God comes upon us by His Spirit?

But we must remember that the power of God becomes manifest through the gifts of the Spirit. This power is not a vague, abstract feeling; it is manifest in good works to man. As Peter says "about Jesus of Nazareth...God had anointed him with the Holy Spirit and with power, and because God was with him, Jesus went about doing good and curing all who had fallen into the power of the devil" (Acts 10:37b-38).

Some say that we should not be interested in miracles and wonders, but that does not agree with what we see in the early church. Stephen, the layman, "was filled with grace and power and began to work miracles and great signs among the people" (Acts 6:8). Philip, another layman,

...Went to a Samaritan town and proclaimed the Christ to them. The people united in welcoming the message Philip preached, either because they had heard of the miracles he worked or because they saw them for themselves. There were, for example, unclean spirits that came shrieking out of many who where possessed, and several paralytics and cripples were cured. As a result there was great rejoicing in that town (Acts 8:5-8).

Even Philip's unmarried daughters prophesied (see Acts 21:9), for the gifts of the Spirit are given to man or woman, young or old, layman or clergy. "In the days to come—it is the Lord who speaks—I will pour out my spirit on all mankind. Their sons and daughters shall prophesy, your young men shall see visions, your old men shall dream dreams. Even on my slaves, men and women, in those days, I will pour out my spirit" (Acts 2:17-18). Jesus told His disciples, "And as you go, proclaim that the kingdom of heaven is close at hand. Cure the sick, raise the dead, cleanse the lepers, cast out devils..." (Mt. 10:7-8). The disciples, and the Church afterward, faithfully carried out this command.

Irenaeus, one of the Church fathers of the second century, wrote in defense of Christianity, saying, "Some drive out demons really and truly...some have foreknowledge of the future, visions, prophetic utterances; others, by the laying on of hands, heal the sick and restore them to health; and before now, as I said, dead men have actually been raised and have remained with us for many years."[4] If that was the Church of the fourth century, then we can see

---

4.   Francis MacNutt, *Deliverance From Evil Spirits* (Grand Rapids, MI: Chosen Books, 1995), 132.

what we have lost. While Jesus told His followers to proclaim His power and authority, and prove it by their works, we often proclaim our powerlessness by our doctrine, and prove it by our helplessness. But the Spirit of God has come to make Jesus real in us again for, "Jesus Christ is the same today as he was yesterday and as he will be for ever" (Heb. 13:8). It is by the power of the Spirit that we can again begin to fulfill the wonderful words that Jesus spoke of Himself. "The spirit of the Lord has been given to me, for he has anointed me. He has sent me to bring the good news to the poor, to proclaim liberty to captives and to the blind new sight, to set the downtrodden free, to proclaim the Lord's year of favor" (Lk. 4:18-19).

And we will be able to do what Jesus told us to do. "I tell you most solemnly, whoever believes in me will perform the same works as I do myself, he will perform even greater works... " (Jn. 14:12).

If such power is available for us, we may ask how we are to receive it. I believe the pattern is set for us right after Pentecost when St. Peter tells how others might receive what the 120 had received. " 'You must repent,' Peter answered, 'and every one of you must be baptized in the name of Jesus Christ for the forgiveness of your sins, and you will receive the gift of the Holy Spirit' " (Acts 2:38). Therefore, the order should be:

1. Repentance and faith in Jesus Christ as our Savior;

2. Baptism and the cutting off of the old life;

3. Receiving the Holy Spirit and power.

What a difference there would be in the church if this pattern were followed. But God is willing to give us His gifts even if He has to change the order that is suggested. To meet the needs of the Gentile converts, He filled them with the Holy Spirit before they were baptized in water. He will also be glad to meet us at our point of need.

First, it is necessary that we personally receive Jesus Christ as our Lord and Saviour. Then, it is very important that we be set free from the old life so that we will not be dragged down by it. Then, we may ask, and receive, the Holy Spirit for power in our lives. The baptism with the Holy Spirit is not accomplished for all at Pentecost; but as we individually receive Christ as Saviour, we are also to receive the Holy Spirit for power. Peter said, "The promise that was made is for you and your children and for all those who are far away, for all those whom the Lord our God will call to himself" (Acts 2:39). Since we are part of "all who are far away," we may also receive the fulfillment of that promise given by Jesus when He said, "Whoever drinks this water will get thirsty again; but anyone who drinks the water that I shall give will never be thirsty again: the water that I shall give will turn into a spring inside him... " (Jn. 4:13b-14). He was speaking of the Spirit, which believers in Him would receive later. Just as for salvation we receive Christ and salvation becomes ours, so also, for the gifts of the Holy Spirit, we receive the Holy Spirit and His power is ours.

Let us look into the New Testament to see how men and women received the baptism of the empowering of the Holy Spirit. In the first instance recorded, the Spirit came at a prayer retreat (see Acts 1 and 2). Jesus had told His followers not to leave Jerusalem until the Holy Spirit came upon them with power. We do not know how many followers Jesus had; though we know that over 500 saw Him after His resurrection. But of all His disciples, only

120 decided to do what He told them to do. These met to-gether to wait, and undoubtedly to pray. Jesus had not told them how long they would have to wait, but after waiting a whole week and nothing happened they did not give up. They seemed to be determined to wait until God's promise was fulfilled. It took ten days, but we know that they were abundantly rewarded. How thrilled they must have been when they saw 3,000 people come to Christ in one day. What a change from their former experience!

This illustrates one of the basic requirements to be filled with the Holy Spirit—namely, that we stay with God's promise until it is fulfilled. There is no time limit with God, but it may well take time for God's cleansing action to remove the barriers of unbelief and fear so that we can receive His great promise. Therefore, we are to wait in ex-pectation for God to fulfill His promise, for He has clearly told us that we are not to try to witness without the power of the Holy Spirit.

Another way of receiving the Holy Spirit's baptism was by the laying on of hands. When Philip preached in Samaria, he did so with miracles accompanying his minis-try and many were saved and baptized (see Acts 8). Then Peter and John came and laid hands upon them, and they received the Holy Spirit. Some people say of themselves that they received the Holy Spirit when they were saved and do not need to ask the Spirit to come again. It is per-fectly true that to be saved we are born of the Spirit, and if we are saved we have the Holy Spirit (see Rom. 8:9). But it is one thing for the Spirit to bring about regeneration, or the new birth, and quite another to have Him bring power for ministry. Peter and John recognized that the believers in Samaria did not yet have the Holy Spirit in power, even though they had believed and were baptized, so they laid their hands on them and the Spirit came upon them.

Some receive the baptism of the Spirit very simply in faith, but some find great difficulty. If we have prayed, but not received such power as the Holy Spirit gives, we may well ask that hands be laid upon us by those who have been filled by the Holy Spirit. Through their faith, along with ours, we may be able to receive the Spirit in power in our lives. Note that it is not the importance of the person who lays his hands on us that counts, but the reality of his experience and his faith. Peter and John came to lay hands on the converts of Philip's ministry, but the Lord sent an unknown, Ananias, to lay hands on Saul to be filled with the Holy Spirit so that he could become the great apostle Paul.

Some, however, may not be so fortunate as to have the help of others. They may be in a church where these things are not taught or encouraged. These people may be encouraged by the experience of the believers as recorded in Acts 10. In this case, the preacher (Peter) did not want his hearers (the Gentiles) to receive the Holy Spirit, but God poured out His Spirit upon them, because He knew that they were ready. If you know that Jesus has commanded that you are to be baptized with the Holy Spirit and you prepare yourself in faith, God will be faithful to His promise, in spite of all opposition. However, note that it will be necessary for you to allow the manifestation of His gifts in order to experience His power as the Gentile believers did.

There is another instance given to us that may illustrate how we may be filled with the Holy Spirit (see Acts 19). The apostle Paul came to the city of Ephesus and found a group of disciples. He evidently saw that they were power-less in their witness for Christ, for he asked them if they had received the Holy Spirit when they believed. It is inter-esting to note that Paul here, and Peter and John earlier, expected the believers to be filled with the Holy Spirit. Earlier than that, John the Baptist pointed out that the great thing that Jesus would do is to baptize His followers with the Spirit.

Now when the disciples in Ephesus said that they did not know about the Holy Spirit, Paul told them to believe in Jesus and then he baptized them. As Peter had pointed out before, faith in Christ and baptism for the remission of sins normally precede the receiving of the Holy Spirit.

In this day, many see the power of God in the healing of a loved one or the freeing of one addicted to drugs. They desire to have such power to help others, but they themselves have never yet been saved. If their desire for power is not selfish, but comes out of pure motives, then they can be assured that they, too, can know the power of the Holy Spirit, provided that they repent, believe in Jesus, and are baptized. Often when people are prepared with this expectation, they are filled with the Spirit as they come out of the waters of baptism.

The key to the baptism of the Spirit lies in believing the promise that Jesus made as He said,

> *"If any man is thirsty, let him come to me! Let the man come and drink who believes in me!" As scripture says: From his breast shall flow fountains of living water. He was speaking of the Spirit which those who believed in Him were to receive...* (John 7:37b-39).

We may ask Jesus to baptize us with His Spirit as we are alone, or we may ask for the help of others. But we can be assured that He will meet our heart's cry, even if others do not understand.

Why then have some sought so long for the power of the Spirit and not found it? Many have accepted Christ in faith and been born into the family of God. Many, also, have believed that they have yielded their lives to the Holy Spirit but, sometimes unconsciously, there were reservations. Some have had doctrinal reservations. They wanted the Spirit of God to work only in the way that they had learned from their church doctrines, and therefore not according to the ways that the Holy Spirit truly manifests himself. Therefore, He could not give His power. Some have had reservations about surrender. Since God may work contrary to rational thought, which might be foolishness to men, they have been afraid to yield themselves fully to Him. The Spirit of God will never force His way upon people, so they were left with their own wisdom and without the power of God. There must be a full, unconditional surrender to God for Him to work in and through us, as He will, before He can fill us with His Spirit. Let us remember that He is the Spirit of the Eternal God, infinite in wisdom, and power, and love. Let us be very careful lest we try to use the Spirit's power to our own advantage; rather, let us cleanse ourselves from all sin, especially the great sins of pride and unbelief, and so, yield ourselves to Him for His great purpose. We are not to decide which gifts we are to have, but we are to be subject to the Lord, the Spirit. "All these are the work of one and the same Spirit, who distributes different gifts to different people just as he chooses" (1 Cor. 12:11). As we remove all barriers, God will be faithful to His promise to us.

We are left with the command, "Be filled with the Spirit" (Eph. 5:18b). It is not a matter of choice, but we are under orders from the One who rescued us from the kingdom of darkness and brought us into the Kingdom of Light. However, if we are to deal with the power of God, we must be set free from the fears and bondages and hurts of the old life. We must learn to listen with our whole being to God, for He speaks to us not only through our rational thought, but by His Spirit, through the Word and in the deep realms of the unconscious, as He communicates with our spirit. As we yield to God, His Spirit will fill us with power and wisdom.

Questions for Discussion

1. What are the prerequisites to receiving the baptism with the Holy Spirit? What is the cost involved?

2. How are the gifts of the Spirit and the fruit of the Spirit related?

3. What are the primary results of the baptism of the Spirit in the believers' lives?

Epilogue

Now that the Holy Spirit has led us into these experiences, can we go back to the frustration of trying and failing in our own strength? Can we again say that the gifts of the Spirit are not for today after we have seen and felt the power of God through them? Is the shame too much to be identified with those who speak an irrational, though heavenly language, or the cost too great when we are cut off from relationships that are dear and familiar?

No, never, never, when once we know the wonder of God that thought the shame was not too much nor the cost too great for Him to use us, who had once been rebel creatures, to do His work in His own Son's name. Suddenly, those once-feared gifts of the Holy Spirit become an amazingly beautiful expression of the life of Jesus himself.

It is indeed a living, loving way.

Order Form

Books

☐ Learning to Hear God's Voice .... $ 7.95

☐ Dreams: Wisdom Within.. $14.99

☐ Dream Interpretation:
A Biblical Understanding.. $ 8.99

☐ Dreams: Giants and Geniuses in the Making........ $ 5.99

☐ Christian Maturity:
How to Flow in the Gifts of the Spirit .... $ 8.99

Video and Audio Tape Series

Casette tapes covering the same material as this book are available. The album contains 8 tapes for $35.00. Order the "Christian Maturity and the Spirit's Power" cassette album. See order form on back pages.

Christian Dream Interpretation
☐ 22 Half Hour Video Lectures $65.00
☐ 11 Hours of Audio Tapes...................................... $49.00
☐ Study Manual.. $ 6.95

Spiritual Principles Involved in Psychogical Counseling
☐ 12 Half Hour Video Tape Lectures $45.00
☐ 6 Hours of Audio Tapes.. $35.00
☐ Study Manual.. $ 4.95

Christian Maturity: How to Flow in the Gifts of the Spirit
☐ 8 Hours of Audio Tapes.. $35.00

Above are U.S. prices for 1997.

Direct all orders and inquiries to:
Herman H. Riffel
2015 Stone Ridge Lane
Villanova, PA 19085

Phone: (610) 527-5389
Fax: (610) 527-1488
E-mail: RiffelH@icdc.com

U.S. Postage and Handling (per item):
Books.. $1.50
Tape Albums $3.00

Please include cost of postage and handling in your order payment. Thank you.

Name_____

Address_____

City _____ **State** _____ **Zip**_____

Destiny Image
Revival Books

HIS MANIFEST PRESENCE
by Don Nori.
This is a passionate look at God's desire for a people with whom He can have intimate fellowship. Not simply a book on worship, it faces our triumphs as well as our sorrows in relation to God's plan for a dwelling place that is splendid in holiness and love.
Paperback Book, 182p. ISBN 0-914903-48-9 Retail $7.99

PRAYER AND FASTING
by Dr. Kingsley Fletcher.
We cry, "O God...bring revival to our families, our churches, and our nation." But we end our prayers quickly—everyone is hungry and we must eat before our food gets cold. Is it any wonder that our prayers are not prevailing? Discover the benefits of prayer and fasting...and learn to fast successfully.
Paperback Book, 168p. ISBN 1-56043-070-2 Retail $8.99

REQUIREMENTS FOR GREATNESS
by Lori Wilke.
Everyone longs for greatness, but do we know what God's requirements are? In this life-changing message, Lori Wilke shows how Jesus exemplified true greatness, and how we must take on His attributes of justice, mercy, and humility to attain that greatness in His Kingdom.
Paperback Book, 182p. ISBN 1-56043-152-0 Retail $8.99

SECRETS OF THE MOST HOLY PLACE
by Don Nori.
Here is a prophetic parable you will read again and again. The winds of God are blowing, drawing you to His Life within the Veil of the Most Holy Place. There you begin to see as you experience a depth of relationship your heart has yearned for. This book is a living, dynamic experience with God!
Paperback Book, 182p. ISBN 1-56043-076-1 Retail $8.99

Available at your local Christian bookstore.

Internet: http://www.reapernet.com
Prices subject to change without notice.

Destiny Image

Revival Books

WHEN THE HEAVENS ARE BRASS
by John Kilpatrick.

In 1988 Pastor John Kilpatrick wanted "something more." He began to pray, but it seemed like "the heavens were brass." The lessons he learned over the next seven years helped birth a mighty revival in Brownsville Assembly of God that is sweeping through this nation and the world. The dynamic truths in this book could birth life-changing revival in your own life and ministry!

Paperback Book, 168p. ISBN 1-56043-190-3 (6" X 9") Retail $9.99

WHITE CANE RELIGION
And Other Messages From the Brownsville Revival
by Stephen Hill.

In less than two years, Evangelist Stephen Hill has won nearly 100,000 to Christ while preaching repentance, forgiveness, and the power of the blood in what has been called "The Brownsville Revival" in Pensacola, Florida. Experience the anointing of the best of this evangelist's life-changing revival messages in this dynamic book!

Paperback Book, 182p. ISBN 1-56043-186-5 Retail $8.99

PORTAL IN PENSACOLA
by Renee DeLoriea.

What is happening in Pensacola, Florida? Why are people from all over the world streaming to one church in this city? The answer is simple: *Revival!* For more than a year, Renee DeLoriea has lived in the midst of the revival at Brownsville Assembly of God. *Portal in Pensacola* is her firsthand account of this powerful move of the Spirit that is illuminating and transforming the lives of thousands!

Paperback Book, 182p. ISBN 1-56043-189-X Retail $8.99

Available at your local Christian bookstore.

Internet: http://www.reapernet.com

Destiny Image
Revival Books

THE COSTLY ANOINTING

by Lori Wilke.

In this book, Wilke boldly reveals God's requirements for being entrusted with an awesome power and authority. She speaks directly from God's heart to your heart concerning the most costly anointing. This is a word that will change your life!

Paperback Book, 182p. ISBN 1-56043-051-6 Retail $8.99

FORGIVENESS: THE KEY TO DIVINE RELEASE

by Rev. Alfred S. Cockfield.

We need revival today—but revival will come only as each believer faces one of the greatest hindrances to its release: unforgiveness. When we actively forgive others—in both our personal lives and in our local church bodies—healing and revival will come!

Paperback Book, 210p. ISBN 1-56043-826-6 Retail $8.99

A HEART FOR GOD

by Charles P. Schmitt.

This 30-day devotional/study on David's life is packed with insight and instruction. By looking at David's life, we can learn how to deal with circumstances in our own lives. From dealing with broken relationships to finding God's will, this book provides powerful lessons that will change your life!

Paperback Book, 238p. ISBN 1-56043-157-1 Retail $8.99

Available at your local Christian bookstore.

Internet: http://www.reapernet.com

Prices subject to change without notice.